Praise for *Confronting Our Freedom*

These two authors—Peter and Peter—offer us an exposition that will burst open many of our best assumptions and categories of interpretation. They range widely into our economy; they dig deeply into our most intimate and demanding relationships; and they probe honestly into issues that divide and summon our society. The sum of this is fresh thinking about the great gift of freedom and our shared responsibility for the wellbeing of our society. These authors come at issues in fresh ways. It is not a surprise that their judgments result in a profound summons to us.

—Walter Brueggemann,
Columbia Theological Seminary

Confronting Our Freedom: Leading a Culture of Chosen Accountability and Belonging is a book of its time where distributed work and post-pandemic living have ushered in a new set of challenges and opportunities when it comes to how we want to live and work. This book is another foundational work by Peter Block that will serve a new generation of thinkers when it comes to asking the big questions about what is a company and how does it serve in the world.

—Rob Locascio,
Founder and CEO Live Person, Inc

In *Confronting Our Freedom*, Peter provides a radical departure from organizational life as we know it. He invites us to deconstruct long-held practices and ways of being in the workplace that prioritize control, predictability,and an unhelpful relationship between leader and employee. Many of these practices we in Human Resources have created and perpetuated with the best of intentions. After reading Confronting Our Freedom, I am inspired to reimagine how different our workplaces could be when we believe freedom is inherent in every person and accountability is chosen rather than induced. This is a must-read for everyone practicing human resources in today's workplace.

—Tonya Harris Cornileus,
PhD, Senior Vice President, Learning & Talent Solutions,
The Walt Disney Company

Peter Block has a unique gift: to invite each of us to imagine a different future and then he inspires us to do what we need to do to co-create that future. My hope is that *Confronting Our Freedom* will ignite a global conversation toward a new narrative around leadership and organizations. What if we took these ideas seriously? What if we could figure out how to dismantle taken-for-granted and often oppressive structures, processes, and ways of working and work together to co-create organizations with freedom at the core? I hope that many will be inspired to read this book, join the conversation, and do what they can to co-create a more just and equitable world.

—Louise van Rhyn, DMAN
Founder, Partners for Possibility

Confronting Our Freedom is the philosophic foundation from which a new social contract and architecture can emanate. It is a guide to social alchemist and architect alike. Our understanding of how to reclaim our capacity to create the world we inhabit can be found its pages.

—Peter Pula
Founder, Axiom News and Convenor,
Cultivating the Great Community

This is an insightful book about restructuring the world for freedom and collective accountability. It reminds us of the habits we are resigning from and a new meaning for accountability in our lives.

—John McKnight
Cofounder, Asset-Based Community Development
Institute, author of *The Careless Society*, coauthor of
Building Communities from the Inside Out,
The Abundant Community, and *An Other Kingdom*

Peter Block is the quintessential collaborator—who brings out the best in his colleagues, companions, clients, and friends. This is especially true in *Confronting Our Freedom* where he teams up with the existential philosopher of commerce Peter Koestenbaum to examine the ideas and practices we most need to re-invigorate our post-pandemic era. The result is an inspiring invitation to go deeper into the meaning of exactly what it is we do in our work lives, why and how we do it, and what it ultimately means to ourselves, our world, our posterity, and the earth.

—Robert Inchausti
Author, *The Ignorant Perfection of Ordinary People* and *Spitwad Sutras: Classroom Teaching as Sublime Vocation*

I often ask, "What has COVID taught us about living well?" This book answered that question for me in surprising ways. There is profound wisdom in these writings and the thoughts shared. Freedom is a choice, as is belonging. A better way of living at work and in the world is possible and it starts within. Do take the time to read this book.

—Paul Born
Cofounder, Tamarack Institute and author of *Deepening Community* and *Breakthrough Community Change*

These are prophetic voices of freedom that humanity and the world of organizing and work need today! The Peters are serving up a provocative portion of "philosophic insight" with the intent to place us each at the center of our own lives and institutions. *Confronting Our Freedom* captures the essence of freedom and its natural presence in our lives, a personal freedom, as a "profound way of thinking" about *us* that both Peter Block and Peter Koestenbaum have called forth in their work. Both complex and elegantly simple, they share that "our will is free" and all that may mean. Through the exploration of this freedom we each hold, they ask us profoundly what are we willing to be account-able for? A question that serves as an invitation to the power and free will of our own life, and the future we choose to create.

—**Gary Mangiofico, Ph.D.**
Executive Professor of Leadership and
Management, and Academic Director, Pepperdine
University, Graziadio Business School

With the powerful, philosophical, and provocative ideas in *Confronting Our Freedom*, Peter and Peter invite us to take what we thought was peripheral and bring it to the center of our awareness, to shift from con-sidering freedom as an escape from fears, constraints, burdens, and limi-tations to understanding freedom as the opportunity to be the creator in the unfolding of our own lives, replete with the anxiety that will entail!

—**Charles Holmes**
CE Holmes Consulting, Inc.

It is a daunting challenge to capture the brilliance and importance of what Peter has written in this latest book. He provides a way forward from being stuck personally and organizationally, but only if we have the courage and insight to take responsibility for our choices and accept the anxiety that goes along with being free. *Confronting Our Freedom* is a practical and at depth a spiritual call to reflection and to authenticity that we so urgently need in our lives and for the organizations we serve.

—**Ward Mailliard**
Founding Member of Mount Madonna Center

CONFRONTING OUR FREEDOM

Selected Works
Also by Peter Block

An Other Kingdom: Departing the Consumer Culture, with Walter Brueggemann and John McKnight

Community: The Structure of Belonging

The Abundant Community: Awakening the Power of Families and Neighborhoods, with John McKnight

The Answer to How Is Yes: Acting on What Matters

Flawless Consulting: A Guide to Getting Your Expertise Used

Stewardship: Choosing Service over Self-Interest

The Empowered Manager: Positive Political Skills at Work

The Flawless Consulting Fieldbook & Companion: A Guide to Understanding Your Expertise, with 30 Flawless Consultants and Andrea M. Markowitz

Also by Peter Koestenbaum

Freedom and Accountability at Work: Applying Philosophic Insight to the Real World, co-authored with Peter Block

The Language of the Leadership Diamond® (videotape with Peter Block)

Leadership: The Inner Side of Greatness—A Philosophy for Leaders

The Heart of Business: Ethics, Power, and Philosophy

Managing Anxiety: The Power of Knowing Who You Are.

The New Image of the Person: The Theory and Practice of Clinical Philosophy

Existential Sexuality: Choosing to Love

Is There an Answer to Death?

The Vitality of Death: Essays in Existential Psychology and Philosophy

CONFRONTING

OUR

LEADING A CULTURE
OF CHOSEN
ACCOUNTABILITY

FREEDOM AND BELONGING

PETER BLOCK • PETER KOESTENBAUM

WILEY

Published by John Wiley & Sons, Inc., Hoboken, New Jersey.
Published simultaneously in Canada.

For general information on our other products and services or for technical support, please contact our Customer Care Department within the United States at (800) 762-2974, outside the United States at (317) 572-3993 or fax (317) 572-4002.

If you believe you've found a mistake in this book, please bring it to our attention by emailing our reader support team at wileysupport@wiley.com with the subject line "Possible Book Errata Submission."

Wiley also publishes its books in a variety of electronic formats. Some content that appears in print may not be available in electronic formats. For more information about Wiley products, visit our web site at www.wiley.com.

Library of Congress Cataloging-in-Publication Data:

Names: Block, Peter, author. | Koestenbaum, Peter, 1928- author.
Title: Confronting our freedom : leading a culture of chosen accountability
    and belonging / Peter Block, Peter Koestenbaum.
Description: First edition. | Hoboken, NJ : Wiley, [2023] | Includes index.
Identifiers: LCCN 2022044710 (print) | LCCN 2022044711 (ebook) | ISBN
    9781394156092 (cloth) | ISBN 9781394156115 (adobe pdf) | ISBN
    9781394156108 (epub)
Subjects: LCSH: Management—Philosophy. | Leadership.
Classification: LCC HD30.19 .B57 2023 (print) | LCC HD30.19 (ebook) | DDC
    658—dc23/eng/20221125
LC record available at https://lccn.loc.gov/2022044710
LC ebook record available at https://lccn.loc.gov/2022044711

Cover Design: Paul McCarthy
Cover Art: Courtesy of Jim Block
Printed and bound by CPI Group (UK) Ltd, Croydon CR0 4YY
C004592_221222

To Ari Weinzweig. An entrepreneur who understands that philosophy and enterprise are one and the same thing.

Note to Readers

About how to put the ideas in this book into practice

A more specific methodology for the path toward distributing agency and choice can be found in a series of videos and podcasts at https://www.peterblock.com/the-six-conversations/ and https://www.peterblock.com/interviews/common-good-podcast/.

About Peter Koestenbaum's quotations

Material quoted from Peter Koestenbaum throughout is taken from two previously published books. Sources for the quotations are identified in text as follows:

1978   *The New Image of the Person: Theory and Practice of Clinical Philosophy* (Westport, CT: Greenwood Press, 1978).

1971   *The Vitality of Death: Essays in Existential Psychology and Philosophy* (Westport, CT: Greenwood Press, 1971).

Contents

Contents

Preface

Twenty years ago, the first version of this book rested at the intersection of philosophy and leadership in a practical world. That effort was organized around the voice and thinking of Peter Koestenbaum, an existential philosopher who, after decades of teaching and writing about life and death, vision and reality, turned his attention to the business world. As his attention shifted to business leadership, "The Leadership Diamond" and its variations were published. The cornerstone of this philosophy was the idea that freedom, with its innate appeal and risks, was an essential aspect of being human. And that how we organize work and institutional life was a major player in encouraging or setting limits on our freedom.

Now the world has caught up with the philosopher. A post-pandemic world no longer whispers about freedom. No longer thinks freedom has to be postponed, waiting to be purchased by making your number. Or waiting for the empty nest or counting the years to retirement.

The pandemic gave many more people a taste of not going to a workplace. Technology has long made working at a distance commonplace. People in notable numbers are torn about going back to their workplace. Many of those wanting to keep their jobs do not want to return to the office. Some companies, in turn, are forcing employees to return to the office. It is complicated.

This book rests on the ideas of freedom and accountability. Especially how they fit into our ideas and practices that occur in our places of work. It reframes how we think about the common practices that are the essence of most jobs. It is intended to question our management practices. And offer an alternative. It is ultimately a friendly whisper into how we might think about the common practices that are the essence of most jobs. It is in essence a friendly whisper into how we might question our assumptions about consistency, control, and predictability. Even in organizations that rate highly in employee satisfaction. Best places to work and the like.

There resides in the words that follow an invitation toward freedom. Freedom as a pathway to accountability, which is what management, in the end, is after. Words create a world. Personally, and in the work I continue to do with organizations and communities, there remains the confusion between freedom, liberty, license, revolution, and rebellion. "Freedom fighter" poses a world where someone is withholding your freedom against your will. Even more compelling is the idea that freedom, as used here, is what creates real accountability. For our children, our workplace and our community. Structuring our world for freedom is the path to a collective accountability that puts entitlement and certainty in their proper places. And it is possible as we experience the reality we hold in our hands and feel under our feet all that matters, we will shop less, care for the earth more, and extract less.

Today's conventional thinking is little changed since the industrial revolution took hold a few hundred years ago. The industrial revolution, symbolized by the linen mills of Glasgow, was a radical moment where productivity, the speed and cost of making something, became the point. It replaced independent sources of livelihood, access to common land, and a craft culture. It introduced the idea of a labor force and employment. People were driven off the land and into the cities by enclosure. The promise was a middle class where you had your own lace curtains. Management became the way of organizing human effort, and accountability became a way of holding people. It became the rationale for carrots and sticks, motivation, and rewards for compliance and performance. It introduced the idea that manager was cause and worker was effect. Before industrialization, worker was both cause and effect.

The point here is to explore this way of thinking as one construct, rather than the truth about what works. To question what freedom might bring to where we assemble. To remind us that freedom is in our nature. And that it can be put to good use. Eve knew that and she expressed her freedom through cuisine.

Same with accountability. Why isn't this the first choice each of us will make, every day of the week, on everything that matters to us? Perhaps we were born to choose accountability.

Instead of celebrating and naturalizing freedom and accountability, we live in structures and practices and solutions that are a mixture of treading water and living in the habits of monarchy and colonialism. Having endured the pandemic, which exposed our habits that we are resigning from, we are in a moment to create a shift with a central appreciation that our freedom is present and no waiting is necessary.

Prologue: Then Was the Moment

The first version of this book was called *Freedom and Accountability at Work*. It had its spark in an auditorium forty years ago. There have been very few times in my life where I knew at that instant that something in me was going to change. One of those moments was in 1980 during a lecture by a San Jose State professor named Peter Koestenbaum. Up to that moment in my life, I was focused on questions of how to make life work, how to make relationships work, how to make family work, how to make a business work. Questions of destiny, courage, and freedom were vague and off my field of vision. I had considered the experiences of aloneness, anxiety, and my wounded-ness as my own unique problems. I treated these as problems to be endured or therapeutically or spiritually solved. At that moment I heard Peter name these "problems," and he suggested that I was human, not broken. This shifted something in me that is still in motion.

In this moment of searching for meaning and connection in the midst of great uncertainty, what it means to be human might give us guidance in rethinking our conception of office,

xx   Prologue: Then Was the Moment

workplace, leadership, and management. This is what motivates me to bring the ideas forward again. Shorter this time. More in my own voice. But the words and philosophy and radical spirit always has Peter at its origin.

> *"The starting point for understanding how philosophic insights can change our lives is to explore the meaning of freedom."*
> — *Peter Koestenbaum (1971)*

> *Whoever hurled the first word began civilization.*
> — *Popularized by Sigmund Freud*

The past is not past

My belief since birth was that a person could overcome their problems with hard work, professional help, and the right amount of guilt and confession. When I met Peter, I was forty and working hard to do just that. I had been in therapy, participated in personal development groups (even conducted them), worked hard on difficult relationships, and thought that at some point in life I would leave anxiety behind and in essence have it together. I was like a male Sleeping Beauty, waiting to be kissed by the prince of self-awareness, perhaps only a short insight away from living happily ever after.

   I thought that my personal family history, parents, siblings, point of view, essentially explained who I was. I knew that the key to relationships was honest and timely feedback (I gave lectures on this). I believed in problem solving and was good enough at it. On the work front, I thought organizations existed to make money, serve customers, and meet their objectives. Work, for me, was a place to build self-esteem, pursue ambition, and try to make a living doing the best I could. With as little stress as possible. Still an issue.

In the course of this one-hour lecture, in Stockholm by the way, all of these beliefs were seriously undermined. This professor took the position that my anxiety, isolation, feeling out of control, helplessness, and inner and outer conflicts were not so much my own unresolved psychological inadequacies, but were permanent qualities of being a human being. It is the human condition. I understood him to say that no amount of treatment, no list of accomplishments, no amount of sincere effort would resolve these experiences. What we experience as personal and individual disquiet is really a universal and collective essence of our being. We are each "wounded at the moment of birth" and rather than treat this as a problem to be solved, it is what makes us human and binds us together. In fact, working on self-improvement and the improvement of others, knowing what is best for others, is what divides us. One force that keeps us apart.

I found those ideas deeply disturbing and compelling, and when the lecture was over, I went right to the front of the hall, found Peter, and asked him if I could come to see him in California. He said, "Yes," and told me how to find him—and that began what is at this point a lifelong effort to reframe much of what I had been taught and had chosen to believe.

My relationship with Peter evolved from being a client of his to becoming a friend and colleague. In the early 1980s, I began to invite Peter into the consulting world where I lived

and introduced him to all my clients. This supported a
direction he had already started to take, and he soon left the
academic world where he had lived for thirty-five years to
commit himself full time to bringing philosophy into the
world of business. He is still at it.

Freedom and Accountability at Work was another step to
widen the audience for Peter's ideas. It was an adaptation of
foundational writings contained in two books he wrote in the
1970s. One was titled *The Vitality of Death,* the other called
The New Image of the Person. Peter's ideas and work have moved
far beyond these earlier books; he has written many others
since then, the most recent ones aimed directly at leadership
in the world of business. Yet as much as I continue to learn
from Peter to this day, I still find myself drawn to the more
fundamental ideas of philosophy that these early books defined.

What lies ahead

Today, with a pandemic on our resume, with wealth disparity
at an all-time high, with social media giving voice to our
shadow with unimaginable intensity, and where you do your
work up for grabs, it is the time to reach back and bring the
essence of philosophical insight into our contemporary
thinking about what it means to live in today's world. The
conventional wisdom most of us now operate from is based
on a belief system articulated by the economist, engineer,
game designer, and artificial intelligence programmer. The
problem is that we have spent and consumed much of the
value these disciplines have to offer us, and much of what we
call "new" is really a recycling through ground we have been

walking on for at least one hundred years. We have experienced the promise of technology, and its convenient delivery system, to increase happiness, beauty, and customer satisfaction.

Philosophy offers the possibility of providing new ways to explore old ground. While the discipline of philosophy has been developing for much of the last century and a half, it has not found its way into practical life, or into organizational life, and we need a deeper and more profound way of thinking about what we are doing. The philosophy has been present all along; hopefully the listening is more present.

A gentle warning: This is not an easy exploration for many of us. Philosophy takes us into a realm of constructs and language that many of us are less familiar with. The language of philosophy is an example of its own content, its own point of view. It is not the language of the engineer and economist, or the influencer. It places meaning and experience first, and utility and practical action as a follow-on. As you read on, suspend your need for precise definition; the ideas are meant to be absorbed and felt. As you continue to read, they will work on you; you do not have to work on them.

Peter's ideas work on us by continually recycling the ideas about freedom, accountability, anxiety, death, and suffering—much as we circumambulate an ancient cathedral, or labyrinth, or temple. Each time we walk around, or in this case, read the words drawn from his work, we gain a deeper understanding of their implications and their value. My experience with Peter over these years is one of occasional frustration—I often have no idea what he is talking about. Then, just as I am about to give up, I hear or read a sentence that is golden. It stays with me, it changes my way of thinking about something that matters. It is patience rewarded, a form of alchemy where the lead of my confusion is turned into the gold of my heightened consciousness.

Let me give a sample of those ideas that have been tattooed on my brain:

> "Let me warn you, that if you argue with me, I will take your side."
>
> When I asked him why there is so much suffering in the world, he said "That's a conversation with God."
>
> When I was despairing at my failure in a marriage, he said, "that experience was just an apprenticeship for what is to come."
>
> The one that shifted everything: "Anxiety is the price you pay for your freedom."
>
> "The difficulty with reading a German philosopher is you have to read well into the second chapter before you can find the end of the first sentence."

Philosophy is something you wake up to, not something you quickly get and apply. In this world of speed and convenience, this is a significant shift. The willingness to engage these ideas fully, with some fragile trust and faith, is, in itself, the experience of our freedom. Freedom, in its deepest sense, means that we are writing and creating the book that we are reading. In this form of co-creative reading, we choose to understand what we read, despite our feelings or confusion at the moment. Freedom is the choice to be uncertain. To be a primary agent of our own experience. To understand ourselves and to have the courage to live with all the implications and hope and futility that this entails. To be the creator in the unfolding of our own life. Peter has said in a hundred ways that the cost of freedom is anxiety. Not a great value proposition.

We have been immersed in the narrative of the consumer culture and its organizations for a long while. One of the origin stories is from Adam Smith, who in 1776 declared that his butcher needed to make a profit to create an incentive to cut his meat. This echoed philosopher John Locke, who said that God himself considered it a divine obligation to maximize productivity on every acre of land (Wood, 2017). To not do so would be a sin against God. These and more have exploded our affection for wealth, growth, extraction, disruption, and the cyber world.

The hope for this book is to shift our lens. To take small but clarifying steps in shifting what might be our distorted view of the nature of freedom. To distinguish it from liberty and license, contribute to the shifting of this thinking, and offer a way to see our world and our own experience through the lens of philosophy. We hope to make this shift through you, the reader. We invite you to join in this conversation about freedom and accountability, to find interest in a discussion about the value of anxiety, the life-giving force of death, and the motivating inevitability of evil and guilt. These subjects are our friends and are potential gifts, not burdensome liabilities. They help us see more clearly our own face, bring what we thought was peripheral into the center of our awareness, and help us find some peace in our own existence.

—Peter Block
September 2022

Introduction: The Philosophic Insight

What we are about to explore is a realm of ideas that are as elusive as they are important. They deal with our way of experiencing our lives, something that is so ingrained and foundational that most of us are unaware of the nature of this experiencing. It is like trying to look at your face without a mirror. Narcissus falling in love with his own image in a pond and not knowing it was him. You go through the day, knowing your face is there, visible to the world, but you alone cannot see it. These ideas can also be thought of as being like peripheral vision: You look at something, say a picture on the wall, and on the edges of your field of vision are images that are definitely there, but difficult to see definitively and clearly. No matter where you look, there are always images on the periphery that you cannot quite tie down. The classic description of the elusiveness of these ideas is that they are so much a part of us that to see them clearly is to be a blind man searching in a dark room for a black cat that is not there.

This is the realm of philosophy. Philosophy not only has to deal with that aspect of life that is difficult to grasp, but it is a discipline that has created its own specialized terms. So much so that if you study philosophy, you spend much of your time on the definition of words you will never use frequently. All the time wondering why these words and what they are trying to describe even matter. There really is a world in a word.

The intention here is to bring a set of ideas—namely philosophy, or more specifically existential philosophy— into the real day-to-day world, especially the world of work and relationships and community. To simply understand this philosophy, let alone make use of these ideas, we would normally be required to understand what is meant by *phenomenology, existentialism, consciousness, being,* and more. These are difficult concepts to grasp, made more so by the fact that much of what philosophers have written has been written for other philosophers or for students in a philosophy class. We don't need to define these terms. We only need to watch for their occurrence.

> *"The central tenet of existential philosophy, and this book, is the unequivocal conviction that every person's will is free. Our freedom, in certain areas, is boundless. In this respect, the stance expressed in this book, which is commonly called existentialism, stands in stark opposition to the prevailing winds of doctrine. The belief that dominates western thinking is that we are not completely free, but are a product of our culture, our upbringing, and our genetic composition. If our will is completely free, then it must [be chosen as an alternative to] these other powerful influences."*
> — *Peter Koestenbaum (1971)*

Conversations on freedom and accountability

We do want to make the ideas of existential philosophy more easily accessible to us all. This book is written for those of us who see the limitations of our habitual caring more about living well and productively in the world more than we care about understanding the nature of being alive. It is written for those who are caught in our care about actions, not the bases that underlie our actions. It takes us into conversations about ideas such as freedom, anxiety, death, and guilt—ideas that we may talk about in moments of reflection, or often in times of crisis—but usually we try to avoid them or we approach them with great caution. In fact, we spend more energy trying not to think or talk about these questions than we do trying to figure them out. We typically get interested in these ideas and questions only late in life when our future is mostly behind us.

"We do not rejoice over the total freedom that we possess, but, on the contrary, make great efforts to hide it from ourselves."
— *Peter Koestenbaum (1971)*

We have lumped these conversations under the rubric of "confronting our freedom and choosing accountability." These are concerns we need to talk more about, know more about, and take seriously earlier in life, while we are in the midst of creating the drama of our lives, rather than looking back on it. We have focused on freedom and accountability because our most common ways of thinking about them do not serve us well. We think that freedom is associated with doing what we want, feeling happy much of the time, and in general living an unburdened existence. A false mixture of liberty, license, and entitlement. A vivid example of this is that we think winning the lottery will help set us free. We believe that if we had a different boss, or labored in another workplace, we could more fully experience our freedom. If we had the right mayor or social service support we would be safer, we would find life easier. And we think that much of what we care about can be outsourced. This version of freedom is too narrow and is based more on a marketing illusion than our experience of the real texture of life. Maybe the pandemic and the seeming volatility around us occurs to cause us to be serious about all of this.

We also have a small way of thinking about accountability. We think that people want to escape from being accountable. We believe that accountability is something that must be imposed. We have to hold people accountable, and we devise reward and punishment schemes to do this. We keep clarifying roles, targets, and outcomes as ways to combat challenges.

These beliefs that are so dominant are difficult to question, yet they are the very beliefs that keep us from experiencing what we long for and producing a world we want to inhabit. As long as we believe that our freedom and well-being are dependent on an absence of problems, on our economic situation, and on the actions of those we work for and live with, we are in trouble. We are particularly vulnerable when we believe that great leadership is needed for the world to work.

And as long as we think accountability is reluctantly chosen and thereby requires force to bring it into being, we are unintentionally creating a breeding ground for entitlement. When others try to hold me accountable, I double my efforts to claim what is mine and to be given special treatment. "What's in it for me?" organizes how we manage, the work cultures and processes we create, and a consumer mindset of more and more. In reality, the consumer mindset is given continuous life by designing for customer dissatisfaction.

> *"For with freedom comes accountability, with accountability comes guilt, and with guilt comes anxiety. Since our freedom leads to anxiety, it is easier to repress it than to bear it proudly."*
> — *Peter Koestenbaum (1971)*

The view from where we are

Many of our beliefs are embodied by the generators of modern culture, the marketplace, the modern organization, and our ways of thinking about management, predictability, and leadership. Philosophy is really about a universal form of leadership and the possibility open to each person to shape or create an environment that supports the pursuit of meaning and purpose rather than our current obsession with speed, the ease of connection, financial security, material wealth, and a wise and compassionate soul to run things. Or a world where no one runs things. Self-sovereignty perhaps.

The culture

It is by looking briefly at modern life that we begin the dialogue about how to sustain ourselves in the face of the dominant culture and narrative. To bring philosophy into the foreground of a practical life.

The more immersed we become in a changing culture, the more we need to be reminded of what is timeless and fundamental. We live in a culture that measures progress by commerce, by scientific and technological improvement. Today's technology world sees progress as being about the possibilities of the Digital Age. With this electronic revolution, our notions of time, space, and distance shift. My distance from anywhere in the world is now measured by the inches between me and a screen. Time has become a scarcity, and the on-call notion of 24/7 rules our consciousness. Speed has become a value in and of itself, waiting one minute for an app to download seems an eternity.

"Science has given us a magnificent excuse and a sophisticated rationalization to abrogate the dreadful sense of freedom and the painful anxiety of responsibility."
                                        — *Peter Koestenbaum (1971)*

Relationships are now heavily automated. I email and Zoom and text what we used to speak. I have an address book where with the touch of a key I broadcast a message to everyone I know. This modernism, as always, is being driven by commerce and convenience as its value proposition. The person from early years is continually transformed from a human being to a consumer, a target market, and the business world now knows more about my taste and preferences than I do. It is packaged as the joy of like-mindedness. As this electronic connection continues to grow, it is accompanied by scientific achievements. We are on the verge of being able to synthetically replace ourselves, and a computer will soon outperform my brain and match what makes me human: my consciousness and capacity to reflect on my own thinking. Intelligence is now artificial. Very handy.

None of this is new. We have lived into devices for leisure and the convenience of electricity for a long time. All of this is the reality of our culture; it will not fade away and carries with it many benefits for us all. In the face of all this, however, there is an increased need to be reminded of all that is true about being human. At the moment when science and technology are able to replace and even exceed all of what I am able to do, my determination to deepen my uniqueness and humanity will grow stronger. The more control we develop over the material world, the more urgent become the questions "What matters?" "How does my life make a difference?" Not just my work life, but my family and community life.

The individual

In addition to finding ways to balance the power of the culture, we also need to interpret what constitutes a meaningful life in the face of our passion for the practical and engineering question of "What works?" None of this is an argument about the advances in digital and convenient living. It is just that because something is amazing does not mean it is important or decisive.

For the last century our understanding of what it means to be human has been dominated by a focus on our behavior, our needs, our wish to be more effective—in other words by the study and application of psychology and the "social sciences." Our bookshelves are filled with advice and wisdom about "how to" do just about anything: sustain a relationship, raise children, manage people, live forever, develop the habits of effective people, navigate the shoals of midlife crises, and basically get what we want out of life. Plus saving the planet.

> *"The lowliest and the highest of us all possess the power and the importance that is given to us merely through the insight that we are born free and that nothing can change this fact."*
> — *Peter Koestenbaum (1971)*

This focus on what works—our instrumental nature—creates a distraction from the question of "What is the point?" which rises from our human nature. These are very different questions. "What works?" is born of a problem-solving orientation. It is a scientist's and engineer's version of our experience that we bring into our own inner world. In his *Interpretation of Dreams,* Freud said, "The dreams of young children are pure wish-fulfillment and are for that reason quite uninteresting compared with the dreams of adults. They raise no problems for solutions." Dreams are uninteresting; problems are cool. The attention to what works is an expression of our problem-solving approach to life—as if life were a problem to be solved. In a restaurant, it always startles me when the waitperson, looking at my mostly empty plate, asks me, "Are you still working on that?" I thought I was having dinner; I didn't realize I had a job to do.

Even relationships are approached on the basis of how they are "working." We want to know what is the use-value or utility of relationships. No wonder we begin to believe that technology can improve relationships, make them more efficient and effective.

This is where psychology has left its imprint. It has taught us how to condition and modify our behavior for the sake of effectiveness. We have one hundred years of practice in this. The dominance of the question, "What works?" becomes a form of psychic materialism where we measure ourselves on our results, on our effect. It becomes an instrumental view of ourselves. This is deeply reflected in how we have constructed our organizations and workplaces. We have defined management as the cause of the workplace and employees as the effect. It is an instrumental transaction.

Our dominant model of leadership is constructed in this engineering, cause-and-effect vein. We have urged leaders to be role models, have vision, be situational in their treatment of subordinates, and to take responsibility for the well-being of those they lead. Our training of managers reflects this. We invest freely in techniques and skills that improve supervision, that train them to motivate and reward employees in order to achieve organizational outcomes. Employees have been defined as the problem and management is the solution. Employees have become objects. When we "acquire talent," we have made a purchase. We purchase employees. Perhaps this is what activates the question of returning to an office.

Philosophy takes a different stance. It holds leadership as a convener where each person is a participant in organized efforts. It proposes that the day-to-day problems facing us are universal. Inevitable small signposts that tell us that how we absorb and respond to them is today's version of the life we are constructing. Willing or not. They are best viewed as symbolic examples of the larger question facing us. This allows them to become the doorways to our transformation and opportunities to experience our freedom, our strength, and our humanity. We each become subjects, not objects. And we need this kind of perspective. We have become so schooled in the perspective of our past producing our present, called developmental psychology, that we put faith in the popular belief that there are simple answers or seven steps to effectiveness. All the how-to-do-it books have been written, the Bible included. It is a different question to ask why we are doing whatever it is and to look for ways we can experience our freedom regardless of the particulars of our workplace or our fractured world. Viktor Frankl found this in a concentration camp.

> *"Once we have mustered the courage to understand, to accept, and to face fully the absolute existence of our freedom, we will discover that it can give us unequalled power to handle our fundamental problems. To accept and to understand one's free will is to have reached maturity, to have developed the capacity to live life fully. The word existentialist comes from this belief in the factual existence of our freedom."*
>
> — *Peter Koestenbaum (1971)*

Organizations and the evolving workplace

The pandemic, with more workers exiting the office and working more independently, has lifted the veil of whether the traditional office and workplace, most organized by the management functions of planning and controlling work, is our most viable model. This makes a more compelling case for the philosophic insight which calls for accountability to grow out of more freedom and peer connection. Instead of overseeing, creating vision, becoming a role model for the sake of subordinates, and, in essence, taking personal responsibility for the well-being of subordinates, a manager would see the task of management as confronting subordinates with their freedom. We treat those who work for and around us as people who are free and who are creating the world within which they live, including how their expectations fall on the manager as parent and provider of certainty. Our organizations have evoked feelings of disengagement and entitlement. Now we also have to face the widespread sense of isolation that existed long before Covid.

Treating people as a freedom questions the conventional belief that people working in organizations are resources, human assets, talent acquisition targets—objects and products and effects of the culture and the leadership in which they operate. For example, I read some research that tried to attribute the causes of a child's behavior to about 30 percent genetics, 35 percent parental influence, and 35 percent the culture in which they live. When I mentioned this finding to Peter, he responded, "Why is there no acknowledgment of free will?" Perhaps because free will is not amenable to being managed. Or measured.

> *"If we examine our actions and decisions introspectively, we discover they possess a unique and irreducible core which can be described by the phrase 'free will.' The existence of this unique quality described appropriately with the expression 'free will' is an unmistakable fact of our experience.*
>
> *"It is true, of course, that the fact of free will is vague, elusive, and perhaps unclear. However, its existence, its actual presence in experience is nevertheless certain. It is as vague and as certain as anxiety, joy, a toothache, and love. The action exists and manifests itself as a ubiquitous and important fact. The fact of free will is pervasive—we are never without it."*
>
> — *Peter Koestenbaum (1971)*

Parenting is the origin story of management and leadership

Philosophy calls for us to question whether our beliefs about child rearing fits for adults. If we seek partnership instead of parenting, it allows us to remove the projection from our thinking about leadership. This means we question the social contract in the workplace that has been organized around good parenting. We have continued to explain employee behavior by examining its management. We hold managers responsible for the morale and productivity of their subordinates. We hold top management responsible for the culture and values they create for others to live in. Management and culture are cause, and employees are effect. Management and culture are subjects and employees are objects. Parents are cause and children are effects. Even when you have several children and see how unique and different they are. The basic contract has been the employee behaves well and they will be taken care of.

> *"Most of us repress the consciousness of that freedom and, conversely, the recognition and utilization of that freedom can give us the power—in fact, that is the only source of power—to make our lives mature, meaningful, successful, and happy, or, in a word, authentic."*
> — *Peter Koestenbaum (1971)*

The pandemic *is* proof that what we thought was true about the office we now just see as an option or a habit. That service employees are low-cost commodities. If we began to believe that employees are "walking freedoms," accountable for creating the world in which they live, it would change many of our ways of dealing with them. For one thing, it would take the monkey off the back of the managers to develop, nurture, grow, and guide their subordinates. If people want mentors, let them find them. If people want to learn and grow, let them organize their own apprenticeships and find their own teachers. If workers want to find purpose in what they do, let them construct a larger sense of whatever we do for a living: programming code, constructing the walls of a building, serving a customer. Seeing a larger purpose is a small step in imagining a future that works for all. Every job we do, including living a prison term of twenty years, can have a larger meaning. The organization committed to confronting its employees with their freedom could support these efforts, but not initiate and institutionalize them, as it now does.

This belief would also reduce the coercive and seductive strategies that now dominate our approach to how organizations should recruit and keep good people. And how organizations change and adapt. As mentioned previously, we would stop the mentality of buying and selling employees, talent acquisition, as if they were just another asset or commodity. Employees would become true partners, instead of partners in name only. We would acknowledge that employees are freely choosing to create this institution, freely choosing to perform well or poorly, freely choosing to blame management or the culture for their suffering. It does not mean that there are no negative consequences for poor performance. It is just that it may not make sense to have our concern for people not fulfilling their promises be the overriding concern for how we come together. This might lead us to the insight that the employees we most want to keep are the ones who will not stay for the money. The term "retention bonus" has within it the seeds of its own limitation.

We would not stop caring about employees, but we would speak to them in a different voice. We would place aside our paternalistic instinct to take care of them, which includes feeling guilty for not having taken care of them. Our voice would be one of a partner, not a parent. We exchange wants with them. When they ask, "What's in it for me?" we would simply say, "Good question. Not one I can answer." When employees ask what the future looks like for the business or their career, managers would say, "I don't know." Employees then say, "Your response is not meeting my expectations." Manager then says, "I know." Silence. Eye contact.

This way managers free themselves to be themselves, and the role-model yoke would be taken from their shoulders. Managers would have room for the range of human responses and in that way affirm their own freedom. The idea that managers, or us in our lives, are required to meet employee or child expectations can be put to rest.

"Our free will discloses that it is composed of three elements or dimensions. Our free actions are spontaneous—they arise out of nothing. Our free actions are self-determined—they are our own personal, individual creation. And, finally, our free actions are choices among alternatives—that at bottom we always could have acted otherwise. There are three consequences in the quality of our lives stemming from the knowledge of these pervasive characteristics of our freely willed actions.

"First, we achieve a sense of power and importance. We recognize that we are individuals with dignity, that we are people who count. The lowliest and the highest of us all possess the power and the importance that is given to us merely through the insight that we are born free and that nothing can change this fact.

"Second, the fact that free will is an essential constituent of what it means to be human suffuses us with a sense of divine mystery and kinship. We are endowed with a basic similarity to our conception of God, who is, after all, envisioned as a Creator and as one who 'created man in His image.' This characteristic of free will gives us a holy charisma—it makes the heart of our soul or mind, our inwardness, the most precious thing in the universe.

"Third, the understanding of free will gives us a sense of supreme accountability: the willingness to accept responsibility and blame for all of our acts is a central ingredient in an authentic existence."

— *Peter Koestenbaum (1971) (emphasis mine)*

Shifting the historical context

This conversation is meant to enrich our way of thinking—to shift the framework of how we understand our experience, to essentially place us in the first-person perspective in relation to our experience. This shift requires some patience in discovering what is useful and practical in these pages. If we too quickly demand practical solutions and quick applications, we will be destined to continually solve problems in the same inherited context that we always have operated under. In this way, the future will continue to be like the past, even more so—like the joke, "What is the difference between the future and the past?" "Nothing, only the future is much longer."

The ideas here, which we are calling "philosophic insight," are intended to simply shift context from one inherited to one created. For example, my parents grew up in the Great Depression, and my children, when young, were in a period of the Great Progression, i.e., the 1960s to 1980s. Growth, materialism, and wealth the dominant narrative. It led to a time when individuals were upwardly mobile, as always, seasoned with an occasional chance to work at home, with no loyalty to an organization. It was a time when organizations began existing primarily for investors and shareholders. The era where their focus was on customers and employees was passing. By the 1990s, the total quality movement and employee involvement initiatives were winding down. The optic was that these efforts have been internalized and no longer need special attention. In these times, up to the present, we also have lost our trust in government, education, and even the idea of public service. Maybe democracy. Look around the world. The media keeps telling us we are divided. Many have lost their faith in science, and we have vaccine debates.

All of this creates great volatility and, like every time of change, carries great possibilities—the price of which is great anxiety. If we can change the context in which we view anxiety, and even the way we view our mortality or evil in the world, then we are better equipped to manage ourselves when "all that is solid melts into air." In the end, our freedom and our experience of accountability may be all we have to hold on to and that might be enough.

To capture in a nutshell the philosophic insights that will aid this shift:

1. Freedom is a fact of our existing in the world.

"Our freedom, in certain areas, is boundless."
                              — *Peter Koestenbaum (1971)*

2. Accountability cannot be imposed or demanded; it occurs as an inevitable outgrowth of that freedom, for we account for what we choose and what we claim as our own agency in making things work. People do not resist change; they resist coercion.

"[T]he understanding of free will gives us a sense of supreme accountability. . . ."
                              — *Peter Koestenbaum (1971)*

3. As inevitably as the existence of our freedom, we are forced to experience and confront:
   - *Anxiety* over the choices we have made as a result of our freedom and the uncertainty of tomorrow.
   - *Guilt* from having said no to either ourselves (existential guilt) or others (neurotic guilt).

"'I-could-have-acted-otherwise' structure. The affective, or feeling, recognition of that structure is called 'guilt.'"
                              — *Peter Koestenbaum (1971)*

   - *Death* of others, first, and the anticipation of our own, next. Not just our personal condition, but the fact that institutions have a life expectancy.
   - *Evil*, which exists because all persons are free, and it will not go away; it is not solvable.
4. And most important—and this is the unique insight of philosophy—these experiences are what give meaning,

character, and texture to our lives; they are not negatives or failures that a healthy person should move beyond.

5. Finally, when we can accept the above, we realize we constitute the world in which we live, which is to fulfill for many the promise of being created in God's image. And this can be embodied in our day-to-day work, not on weekends and retreats.

Philosophic insight in the world of organized effort

To understand how these insights might be translated from abstractions to facts in our own lives, there are two notions that are essential:

- We want to apply philosophic insights to the world of productivity. The work world if you wish. This includes living in communities that support well-being.
- We are interested in freedom and accountability at the center of organized effort. The organized world.

These intentions address the purpose and requirement of each of us. We all want to get something done, together. This is an offer to address questions about how and whether an in-depth understanding of our freedom changes the way we function. These are questions for the collective as well as the individual. Where much of traditional philosophy is aimed at what it means to be an individual human being, we want to widen the scope to explore how a belief in the primacy of our freedom would impact our institutions, our civic space, being an owner of our communal land, our neighborhood as the wilderness, the actual, physical space where we can claim control over individual and collective well-being.

> *"Our free actions are self-determined—they are our own personal, individual creation. What existential philosophy argues for, then, is a person who never gives up; we are to be people who are always looking to themselves as the genuine source and essential fountain for the improvement of their life situation. In keeping with this line of reasoning, blaming other people or external circumstances for our problems, misfortunes, failures, and meaninglessness is not an insight into the 'true' nature of things, but merely a cheap and eventually ineffectual form of escape. To blame others merely means making a decision to avoid the responsibility which ultimately and inescapably is one's very own."*
>
> — *Peter Koestenbaum (1971)*

Real world, really?

As Robin Williams once said, "Reality, what a concept!" Yet it is often more elusive than we admit. If we want to address the work-and-doing world, often called the real world, then we have to consider what is real and who decides it. When we typically talk about facing reality, it is a call for getting practical, a placeholder for cynicism, dampening down our idealism, or accepting the world as it is, not as we wish it to be. Reality has, in a way, gotten a bad reputation. When we are told to face reality, it is generally to prepare for bad news.

We claim that what is real is what is practical. Facing the "hard stuff," which includes science, engineering, the world of numbers, and the drumbeat of the marketplace under this umbrella. The arena of our humanity, relationships, feelings, vision, and meaning is commonly relegated to the "soft stuff." Hence, we have bought the notion that reality is hard-nosed, an invitation to achievable expectations and in general a dehumanizing energy field that we all are forced to endure.

Perhaps we have it backward. Facing our freedom, and the consequences of doing this, is really the hard work. The real work. Confronting those parts of work life that offer numerical certainty or the ability to accurately predict an outcome are really the softer aspects of our workplaces. We allow others to define reality for us when we accept the engineers' and economists' definition of what is real. Numbers, brain science, and the conventional wisdom carry the reputation of being real, but in fact are just comforting. Maybe the world really was flat until we decided that it wasn't.

What is most real in our lives is not so much the truth about the way the world is, but actually what we know to be true, which is a world defined around our own experience. It is the existence of our consciousness that is most enduring and permanent and therefore real to us. All that happens around us, which we call objective, is open to our interpretation. Another expression is the idea that even history is unpredictable. Barbara Tuchman declared that history is the unfolding of miscalculations. The same events will be seen uniquely by each person who observes them. The engineering or scientific viewpoint, which relies on data and predictability, an evidence-based mindset, at best only pays attention to that part of the story which is amenable to this version of what is real. That is because after collecting all the data we can and applying all of our analytical tools, in every case a choice will have to be made in the face of an uncertain world. For every digital tool there is a human being at both ends. It is in making these choices, which are the moments when our freedom is revealed, that the world becomes real. One impact of the pandemic for each of us is the reminder that any certainty we held onto was an illusion.

Uncertain reality

Our experience becomes real when we acknowledge that something is at risk and the stakes are high. The marketplace symbolizes this for organizations, for it operates without personal preference for who it rewards or punishes. It is a test for our actions and can dictate the survival or death of our institutions. The risk of the marketplace, rather than a being problem, can be seen as a gift. It gives our life meaning; it is a testing ground for our deepest beliefs; it is an arena where we answer basic questions about our survival, our value, our capacity to do something useful. This reality of the marketplace animates our freedom and gives us a canvas on which to display our accountability.

Despite the fact that most organizations have evolved into a collection of boundaries, defined roles, and limitations, freedom is not a stranger to the marketplace. The language we have used for freedom in the marketplace is the term *entrepreneur*. This word captures the act of creating something out of nothing. We talk about the entrepreneurial spirit, which is the institutional counterpart of our individual freedom. A startup operation is a good model for an institutional form that operates with a tolerance for freedom and benefits from a generally shared sense of accountability. And this often succeeds in the real world.

If we are willing to accept that beginning a venture requires this freedom, we should ask why, once it gets established, our faith in freedom dwindles, and we think that controls are needed, that professionalism must be installed, and rules and regulations must be defined. Why do we believe that you must sacrifice freedom for the sake of scale? Why are we so drawn to worship consistency? Convenience?

The belief in scale and speed and efficiency has a commodifying effect. In the absence of a special consciousness and care, they extract our humanity. And so our workplaces are soon well structured, roles are defined, behavior is prescribed, and what was a startup now becomes a place we call work. Even when, as in a startup, freedom faces the resistance of so-called marketplace reality, we still are quite ready to surrender it. The code for this is "taking it to scale." Scale is the force that commodifies our way of being together.

At work

For the most part, we have not organized our institutions around the viewpoint that freedom is the most valuable way to organize human effort and that accountability grows out of choice, the acknowledgment of that freedom. As mentioned too many times, we are more organized along determinist lines that believe that we are the result or product of our history and our culture and that our behavior needs modification by those around us in order for productivity and collective targets to be achieved. Our question here is whether organizations could be different if they fully accepted that each person is, in fact, a freedom, and that the recognition of anxiety, guilt, death, and evil is essential to creating outcomes that work and produce meaning.

To begin with, we would pay less attention to techniques designed to influence and control other people's behavior. Especially from bosses. We would question the management theory that provides admonitions about the importance of management role modeling, walking one's talk, wandering around, reinforcing desired behaviors, articulating visions, defining strong cultures, and more. Competency models as a form of making humans more trainable and predictable. This all grows out of the belief that human behavior can be replicated and shaped into a replicable model. Once again, management as the subject and employees as the object.

The dominant belief is that behavior is driven by self-interest and its belief in barter. Quid pro quo. What's in it for me? That good management is a set of actions undertaken for their effect, not for their own sake. Role model. Vision. Mission. Values. All good qualities, popular but not powerful. When we care about them for their effect on employees, we are bringing the engineering materialism of the behavioral psychologist into the human relationships of the workplace. It is this link that denies the existence of employee freedom and depends on a theory of accountability that requires a lot of hand-holding and a generous amount of oversight. It is colonialism in action. Frederick Taylorism and scientific management alive and well.

This all carries a passion and belief in high-control systems. The alternative is to understand this all as a socially celebrated and condoned defense against our freedom and the anxiety it imposes. We create high-control environments and justify them with the belief that without controls, collective effort toward a common goal would not be possible. We then seal this stance: we name it reality. "Let's get real" is a conversation stopper. It calls us to the smallest version of what it means to be human. This would shift in a freedom-based leadership, which would encourage a culture of deeper and chosen accountability.

This is not just about the workplace, but it is the guiding principle of how we organize many of our commitments. What we ask of our schools in helping to raise our children. Public schools have a STEM curriculum established by the state education departments and the legislators. It includes standardized tests and all that requires. This strategy is all about standardizing and control. One of the stated intentions of our education system is to socialize our children. We decide how this should be accomplished with little input from the people in the school connecting with the children. It is bringing business management into the raising of a child.

The main intent here is not to argue with the existing thinking about management, for many of these strategies have their advantages. It is just that prescriptive and parental management reinforces employees as objects or effects and then we think they resist "change," which is a code word for more controls. We then give them more prescribed training, more and more attention, boundaries, and performance management. As we explore both how cautious we are about allowing the institutional exercise and existence of our freedom, and what the alternative might look like, notice that there is nothing in the ideas about freedom that argues against the need for structure or the need for controls. The questions are where the controls come from and how we design the alternative structure.

If we long to triumph in the struggle for our own freedom, then are we committed to inventing ways for our freedom to get institutionalized in our construction of the workplace? Who is to say? We take on this task knowing that up to this moment, much of how we construct our collective efforts is based on the colonial and market myth projection that not only are restraints and controls necessary, but that people want it that way. Our institutions have become a place where we are supported in our escape from freedom. And if we choose to escape from freedom, then we have abandoned any real chance for a culture of accountability.

There is a cost to an organization committed to the freedom of its members, and that is the anxiety and seeming unpredictability that this carries. Managers would lose some of the hunting rights that parenting carries with it. We would have to confront our own need for control at a deeper level and, more important, confront our own lack of faith in the possibilities of the people we work with. And ourselves.

We are each afraid of our freedom, and thus we are afraid of the freedom of those around us. Especially when we are in work that has goals, deadlines, boundaries, and an infinite number of restraints.

It is in this paradox, freedom in the midst of restraints, faith in the accountability of others, in the face of a history of disappointment, that the search begins. The question to pursue is whether there is a way of creating a life and a culture of accountability based on freedom and its possibilities, as opposed to the current strategies of creating accountability through inducement and coercion. It is interesting that when we speak of prescribed action, we call it execution.

"The existentialist view holds that we have no choice in the matter of accepting responsibility for the quality of our lives. That responsibility is ours by birth, by virtue of the fact that we are human, in the same sense that our heart is ours by birth. We are in fact responsible for success as well as for failure in life, irrespective of whether we are prepared to accept and assume such responsibility."
— *Peter Koestenbaum (1971)*

The existential understanding

Freedom and accountability are inherent qualities of our existence. They are present all the time and do not have to be nurtured or induced, as much of our culture and institutions believe is required. On the contrary, it takes conscious (or unconscious) effort to create conditions where people do not act accountably, and do not experience the power of their freedom. The struggle to deeply experience our freedom and to live with the weight of full accountability for the world we have created is in itself not a problem to be solved, but rather what can give meaning to our lives.

The most important conclusion to be drawn from these considerations is that what it means to be a person is your creation. The nature of a person, the meaning of human existence, the provenance and destiny of men and women, the essence and definition of us all—all these are not found or discovered; they are invented.

Existentialism holds that you are totally responsible for your life-situation. . . . The realization that this responsibility is total leads, of course, to anxiety—because of the enormous burden—but it leads also to a sense of power and control, since in your freedom you become a genuine creator. . . . In a crisis, we each experience the anxiety that our total freedom brings to the situation. At these moments we are in the role of God having to create a world of values. There is no appeal beyond our own final decision, but we must nonetheless take full personal responsibility. We only resolve the crisis when we take full, deliberate, clear, and conscientious charge of the situation. We make events happen, not allow ourselves to drift into them. We, not fate, became the master of our life. In other words, we mature.

Each person must be reminded that "man and woman are beings who have no excuses." But it must be made clear that total freedom is a sacred fact of life and not a moralistic reproach. Furthermore, those who instill this knowledge of responsibility in others are human too, and must as a consequence assume total responsibility for their impact.

Adapted from Peter Koestenbaum, "The Existential Crisis in Philosophy and Psychology," in *The Vitality of Death: Essays in Existential Psychology and Philosophy*, Westport, CT: Greenwood Publishing Co., 1971 (Originally reprinted with permission from *Explorations*, no. 7: 26–41).

1

The Power and Structure of Freedom

In exploring the nature of human freedom, we are looking at freedom for our own lives and the place of freedom in our institutions. For individuals, the ideas are more easily compelling. *Sovereignty* has a compelling ring to it. If we bring these ideas into an organizational setting, however, they appear more disruptive and radical. As dear as freedom might be to us personally, it is a subject rarely discussed in our institutions.

You might think that in a democracy, we might be concerned with protecting our freedoms in the workplace. There is little, however, in our theories about management or psychology of human behavior that celebrates our freedom or helps us understand its existence and nature. In fact, the opposite is true. We are more likely to focus on ways that management needs to control and channel behavior in a caring, participative, and compassionate way. We think that we are helping people choose to come on board. This treats people exercising their freedom as a problem to be solved and a proposition to be sold. This is true in our institutions and in the society at large.

> *"The attempt to let decisions emerge spontaneously, as it were, from institutions is a widespread contemporary practice which often serves to blur—and thus hopes to escape—the very nature of free will itself. Such an effort often leads to distortion of the most basic human characteristics, to procrastination of necessary decisions, and the dilution of responsibility and of the solutions proffered; it leads to cowardice where courage is essential, or to foolhardiness when restraint is in order."*
>
> — *Peter Koestenbaum (1971)*

The belief that behavior needs to be channeled is ingrained in more than our organizations. For a hundred years since Freud, the behavioral sciences have led us to believe that behavior is determined not by free choice, but by the family, culture, and organizational context into which we were born or find ourselves. This gave rise to parenting as a specialized skill and childhood as a series of development steps. Given these as reinforcements, it is a logical step to act as if the organization has the responsibility to guide its members toward a useful existence. We might call it the child to management pipeline.

Bring in scientific management about the same time Freud was taking hold. In scientific management, Frederick Winslow "Speedy" Taylor demonstrated that if a worker's movements could be broken into discrete actions, these actions could be taught and controlled and productivity increased. This was the early dawning of the idea that management is the driver and cause of employee behavior, performance, and satisfaction. We conduct attitude surveys to determine employee satisfaction and then—with the enthusiastic agreement of the employees—we expect management to do something about it if it is too low. If we want high-performing, satisfied employees, we think we must train managers on how to motivate, inspire, and guide their people. The alternative is to back off the training instinct for a more teachable and controllable workplace. Let go of competency models. Replace these by engaging employees in constructing their own learning. Call them learning circles. Communities of practice.

The philosophical insight that Peter lays out in his writing is important: If we were to take seriously the existentialist view about the human condition, it would shift not only how we organize human effort, but also how we construct the organization practices and cultures of which we are a part.

> *"Free will is an enormous burden—as existentialists have repeatedly pointed out in such phrases as 'man is condemned to be free' and 'dreadful freedom.'"*
>
> — *Peter Koestenbaum (1978)*

Accepting our freedom

Is there no one—regardless of cultural differences or personal beliefs—who does not in some way long for freedom? Yet we often act as though we doubt its existence. We are cautious of exercising our free will in our everyday lives. We demand proof or assurance that we are free, or we retreat into the security of "rationality." Looking for proof of concept.

Our organizations are full expressions of our belief in constraints. We often treat the workplace, which is a human system, as if it were a mechanical system—or most recently, an information, digital, artificial intelligence system. We place great organizational effort into constructing a world of control, consistency, and predictability. We engage in planning that attempts to predict the future, we believe that structure and rewards drive behavior, and we trust that for every problem there is a solution.

We hold this set of beliefs together by focusing on measurement with deep and abiding resolve. This is most clearly expressed in the statement, "What does not get measured does not get done." We believe that if we cannot measure something, it does not exist. The corollary is that if we want to bring something into existence, it has to be defined in concrete, measurable terms. Most often, when faced with an innovative idea, we ask the question, "Where else has it worked?"

This set of beliefs is the engineering mind in action. It leaves little room for valuing the element of surprise, discovery, and creativity. Our holding onto our belief in the rational, explainable nature of existence is a major reason that organizations have such a difficult time changing and adapting. We often feel that if we want innovation or agility, we are better off starting from scratch, from a green field, than to try and change the system we already have.

Reason interferes with change because of its need to predict and control itself. Our change efforts are filled with the language of prediction. We talk about "driving change" as if it were a car. We "cascade change down through the organization," as if it were a Hawaiian waterfall, or "drill down" a new business strategy. The first question in a shift in direction is defining the "metrics" we will use in determining the success of the shift. Next, we decide what new behaviors will be required and then add them to our people-evaluation system and competency models. Finally, we reward the new behaviors. Rewards and measurements are intimate companions and become cornerstones in the engineer's view of how change happens. In this way, change management is no change at all.

The cause-and-effect version of reality constrains us into a utilitarian quality to our thinking. It is a transactional way of being. With ourselves and others. We begin to believe that all our actions have meaning and value only according to their effect, or their results. It leads us away from doing things for their own sake. We even mold our behavior into tactics that work. The emphasis for the person is away from self-expression and toward instrumentality. If something does not show a result—for example, expressing feelings—then we think it is the wrong, or unwise, thing to do. Enough of touchy-feely stuff. This is why so many of us come to believe that we cannot be ourselves and be successful. We role-play to make a living.

This is not to argue against reason and measurement, only to question its pervasiveness and promise. As Peter argues, our belief in reason and longing for measurable outcomes is a choice, not an immutable fact of nature and existence. If we keep our need for control and measurement in perspective—considering it to be a different viewpoint we might hold—it opens us to more possibilities for what organizational life can become. It honors the complexity and creativity of a human system and might nourish this rather than treat it as a problem.

The fundamental insight

In the world of action and results, thinking is often viewed as lost production. In the broadcasting world, if there is silence, it is called "dead air." In many of the training workshops we conduct, participants are sometimes asked to reflect on their own beliefs, to voice their own theories of how things work, or even to analyze some action that has taken place in the room. When this is done, they often comment that it was fun to have to really think for a change, that it has been a while since they were forced to do that. Some even comment that they have not really had to explore new ideas since they were in school.

The practical world does not usually require in-depth reflection; in fact, it is often hostile to it. The claim is made that we do not have time to question and reflect—as if wonder or plain curiosity might harm productivity or were a sign of uncertainty, perhaps even a weakness. We try to marry speed and innovation with the call to "fail fast." This alienation from thought carries a cost. It forces us to keep repeating the way of thinking and acting that brought us here. Covid interrupted all of this. It might bring us into a new social contract with our workplaces.

> *"Of course, should people not choose identification with the social structure, they also choose the consequences of that grave alienation."*
> — *Peter Koestenbaum (1978)*

Peter takes a deep dive into existentialism to identify the basic assumptions about being human that define our freedom. One radical premise is that we have choice over how we view every aspect of our experience and our lives. This goes against most people's experience in organizations and communities. Most of us are keenly conscious of the constraints that surround us. We spend a significant part of our conversations filing complaints about who is at fault, how others need to change, how it was not our fault. In the larger world, this is called investigative journalism. I have always felt that if we really wanted short meetings, we would live by the rule that no one can talk about anyone not in the room.

> *"Fundamental to existentialist theory is the view that the world as it appears to us is our own creation, and we must assume responsibility for it."*
>
> *"Fundamental to existentialist theory is the view that the world as it appears to us is our own creation, and we must assume responsibility for it."*
>
> *"Fundamental to existentialist theory is the view that the world as it appears to us is our own creation, and we must assume responsibility for it."*
>
> — *Peter Koestenbaum (1971)*

Sorry for the repetition. But this may really be the point.

According to this line of thinking, our blame and judgment of others is merely a symptom, as are our feelings of vulnerability. A root cause of the blame, judgment, and complaining is our denial of our freedom. We institutionally deny the fact that each of us—through our actions and our views of the world—is creating the organization and the leadership we are so fond of complaining about. Deciding that I have created the world around me—and therefore I am the one to fix it—is the ultimate act of accountability.

Most managers see the cost of all the blaming and avoidance of responsibility, but their efforts to evoke more accountability tend to reinforce the cost and futility it breeds. We think we can bring accountability into being through rewards, reinforcement, punishment, and even role modeling. These strategies increase the constraints on people, as if accountability were an unnatural act that needed to be taught or induced.

The philosophic stance gives clues to an alternative strategy, one that confronts people with their freedom and treats accountability as an inherent quality that needs more understanding and tolerance than instruction or inducement.

"Our energies will be channeled into fulfilling our responsibilities intelligently rather than in futile attempts to avoid them."
— *Peter Koestenbaum (1978)*

Implications: The forms of freedom

When we decide that supporting freedom is in the interest of our institutions, we shift our thinking about management. Who needs to be managed? Who does the managing? Does control have to be hierarchically engineered or might we find it to be an element of self-governing units, gatherings, and projects? These are not new questions, but our thinking changes in the context of this discussion about freedom. The challenge is to welcome and institutionalize the existence of freedom with as much enthusiasm as we have institutionalized the need for boundaries and the need for constraint. The belief that freedom must be managed and actually feared, as opposed to released, has led us to our current bureaucratic set of practices. Here are some implications of choosing a faith in freedom that up to now we have conferred upon control.

1. Employees do not need to be motivated

The moment we accept that each person is constituting and constructing the world in which they live, we stop thinking that the job of managers is to take responsibility for the morale and motivation of people who work for them. Of course, treat them well and build strong relationships, but end treating motivating subordinates as part of a job description. Human motivation is an individual decision, not an environmental consequence. We currently act as if people are not inherently motivated but instead go to work each day and wait for someone else to light their fire. This belief is common among managers and employees alike. The belief that management is responsible for employee actions is the perfect defense, for each side is quick to blame the other for their disappointments.

It is one thing to hear employees blame management for employees' lack of motivation or poor performance; it is another thing for managers to swallow the bait that they, themselves, are at fault, they are cause, and believe it. We have accepted the idea that managers are responsible for their employees' attitudes and behavior, so much so that in some organizations, managers are evaluated and paid based on employee ratings of their manager. This inversion simply breeds a culture of entitlement.

People are also responsible for their own morale. If employees want to be depressed, then why would we steal from them that right? This is not to deny that there are some managers whom no one wants to work for, who abuse their power and should not be managers. But their employees still have a choice about how to deal with them. They have a choice to stay or leave, to join together to demand a change, to ignore management and get on with the work, or unionize and structurally institutionalize their power.

When top management or a staff group conducts an attitude survey of employees that asks how they feel about management, they collude with the part of employees that does not want to be responsible for their own experience. It legitimizes the idea that employee well-being is in the hands of management. Plus, when top management gets the survey information, it is rare they can find really useful ways to act on it.

It is right and human for managers to care about the motivation and morale of their people; it is just that they are not the cause of it. Managers should stop asking for feedback from employees about how they could improve as managers. If you want to know how another human being feels about you, ask them. Individually, but not in a survey. Ask out of your own interest and desire to learn, not for the sake of your employees. And stop institutionalizing it with 360-degree feedback surveys. If we decide to view employees as free and accountable, then we stop soliciting from them what they are free to express any moment they choose. Freedom and accountability call for the end of fixing each other.

Plus, if we want to hold on to the belief that managers and employees create each other, why do we believe that motivation only flows downhill? Who motivates the managers? Does it make sense to believe that it is the employees' job to be responsible for the morale and motivation of those above them? If a manager is depressed, do we expect their employees to ask what are they doing to depress that manager? Do we ever ask what new skills they need to increase top management's spirits? Not often.

2. Rewards do not explain and drive behavior

The most sacred and widely accepted belief in organizations is that rewards, in the form of praise, shout-outs, and compensation, drive behavior—that people will fundamentally do what is institutionally rewarded. What does not get rewarded does not get done. Touch this belief, and your fingers get burned.

Compensation systems are like a bad marriage. Not happy, but we fear that if we get out of it and look for something better, we might end up worse off than before. So it is with the sacred ground of how we pay people. We have energy about pay that far transcends what you would expect from an economic transaction between employee and employer. Looking at our paycheck, we draw conclusions about self-worth, justice in the world, our political and economic system, and our personal security. The reward systems that most of us live under are a reflection of our enduring class system and our love affair with leadership. The challenge is to create pay practices that support accountability and commitment to the well-being of the whole.

Without getting too deeply into the specifics of compensation, what is relevant here is the belief that instrumental barter is fundamental to our current organizational relationships. We think that the institution must purchase what it wants from people, just as it purchases every other resource. If we want a certain behavior, we have to order it and put money on it. "Pay for Performance" is what it is called. Its cousin is the talent acquisition department. There we act as though talent procured, acquired, names a work relationship without any ambiguity. Welcome aboard, we hope that you will be a fine purchase.

Alternatively, if we accepted that employees are choosing their actions freely and of their own accord—and are thereby choosing the world they want to live in—we would keep barter and pay in perspective. We would put it on a back burner, make it fair and transparent, but not fundamental. It would cease being a universal solvent. We would then stop turning to economic solutions to problems whose source lies elsewhere. We would stop looking at pay as the reason they left.

This would put an end to devices such as golden handcuffs, hiring bonuses, and retention bonuses. We would offer employees stock ownership because it seems right to us since they are actively creating the wealth of the organization, not because it will change their behavior. We might question the elitist distinctions we make by having different pay systems for executives, managers, and workers. One effect would be to disconnect executive pay dramatically from stock price, since there is little hard evidence that this helps create a healthy future for an institution. It makes sense that stock price is a reflection of our collective results and achievements. To heavily weight the distribution of equity bonuses and options to the executives is a distortion of who is producing the results. It is an affirmation of empire and reinforces the myth that executives are cause and all others are effect. Pay the executives more because they carry a heavier responsibility. Pay more to outstanding talent and performers at each level. Keep it in proportion, though, so that rewards are transparent and fair. Not the vehicle for declaring why we have come together.

The specifics, though, are not the point here. What matters is the recognition that human beings cannot be purchased; they are not possessions or assets of the organization that are reducible to simple market transactions. They are not talent to be acquired or purchased. They are not commodities waiting for their work to be automated. And if, despite this argument, it still seems to you as though employees are primarily driven by pay and promotion, then take this as the product of a world you have chosen to construct, a picture you have chosen to paint.

3. The organization does not have to develop "its" employees

When we decide that each employee is a freedom and an accountability by nature, then employee development becomes simply an opportunity for self-definition. It is no longer the responsibility of the organization to develop "its" people. Or to know what is best for them. Even the possessive term "its" implies that the employee belongs to the organization, that the organization owns "its" people. This is a colonial instinct. When we stop possessing people, then our organizations can support learning and have a stake in learning, but not be responsible for it. Each person would be required to choose their own way of learning, define their own learning goals, and figure out how and when to pursue them. Included in this is to identify people in your system that you want to learn with. It is useful if the organization helps to create learning cohorts but let those cohorts struggle with what and how to learn.

Management still has to give feedback to employees, be happy or disappointed in them, but it is the employee who decides what change is needed. The implicit bargain around performance—that if the employee exceeds management expectations, then management will in some way take care of the employee—would disappear. The institution will always make demands, reward and punish individuals, but the rewards do not become a bargaining chip. In reality, rewards and punishment come to each person with the same predictability as the weather: It can make a big difference to us, but the idea that we can control it or ultimately predict it is foolish. This has been made evident with the pandemic. Too many talented people are not returning to the job they once held. There is no simple way to understand this, but it can add to our intention to seek new thinking about the human dimensions of the workplace and this thing called an office.

"What is the frame of mind, the world view, the perception of reality of a person who says that free will does not exist? Or a person who insists on a deterministic and mechanistic world view, that perceives the world as predictable?"
— *Peter Koestenbaum (1978)*

When people are forced to face the reality of their own freedom, and believe that management no longer possesses them, they see that their future is in their own hands. It means that you don't have to "make your number" to do what you want. While the rewards that management has to offer may be of value, they are no longer compelling. They cease to be an excuse for our actions. If I know that my freedom is my birthright—that my future is mine to create—then I will no longer be foolish enough to look longingly at the organization and ask them what I should become. Save that for your parents; don't transfer that to your boss. Stop asking other human beings what they have in mind for you. Ambition gets redefined as a pursuit of individual and organizational purpose, not a pursuit of advancement, progress, or appreciation. And the idea that we would ask the organization to "promote" us would make as little sense as asking your partner in business or in life to "promote" you. We were not our parent's favorite child, and we can live with and perhaps be grateful for our anonymity. If you were the favorite child of whoever raised you, just relax, you will eventually get over it.

This mindset also changes the nature of the training programs we offer. They will demand more participant initiative. Participants will join in defining their goals, constructing the form of the learning, and being responsible for its success. Training will stop being something done to or for the employee, but something done by and with the employee. All are responsible for co-constructing their lives and so also their learning experiences. The idea that people do not know what they do not know is no longer used as a rationalization for high control teaching to supposedly empty vessel students.

Evaluation also is an important bellwether or symbol of our stance on freedom. When we ask people to evaluate a meeting or learning event, we might ask them to evaluate how they themselves did, not how it was managed or whether it was conducted to their satisfaction. Meetings are another space for engaging ourselves in the act of co-creation. If we have an hour together, how can we construct this time to make choice and accountability a central purpose?

If we continue to decide what people should learn and how they should learn it, we will forever have to convince them that learning is good for them. We will continue to sell them on learning, mandate or nominate their attendance, and they, in turn, will act as if learning is an entitlement instead of a privilege. When participants enter the room of a learning event knowing full well that they chose to be there, the social contract of their learning has shifted dramatically. It is no longer up to the instructors to prove their value and relevance; it is clear from moment one that the learners are responsible for what value they receive.

This all is more than a shift in semantics; it is a shift in the social contract. It breaks the parenting bondage. It also dramatizes the cost of our freedom. And we move in this direction not because the employees are asking for it, but because we are committed to the well-being of the institution and to a world based on real life. The existing deal between institution and employee, despite the free agency rhetoric and the distributed workplace, is still based on the unreal belief that the institution owns the employees and therefore is morally and operationally forced to motivate them, reward them, and develop them. More about the social contract later, for remaking this will be an enduring outcome of the pandemic.

One more element of human resources is for us to reassess our thinking about who we hire. We now screen people according to their past. We use criteria that have little basis in fact. We want people who have attended certain schools, achieved certain levels of education, chosen certain rites of passage. Little of this is based on fact; it is more an issue of class. School class and social class. One of the blessings of the Internet revolution is that it has made visible the possibility that people can contribute according to their inherent talent, and not the accident of their family or educational history. This is also the essence of any commitment to social justice and inclusion. Plus we let go of the corporate class. Each industry has its golden companies and culture. Not a good basis for hiring.

All this requires us to face our own faith in the possibilities of unique culture and local choice. We can choose in a minute to live into the hope that we will create chosen accountability to replace the purchased and mandated accountability that drives our conventional wisdom. What reassures me in seeking a different way of thinking is that the current wisdom is not working very well. Our institutions may often seem successful, but they are so despite being a breeding ground for entitlement and passivity, not service and activism.

4. Leadership is abundant, not rare

Leadership is the willingness to initiate the world, to involve ourselves and others in producing what did not exist before. It is the willingness to step into uncertainty. This is the exercise of freedom, which means that leadership includes the task of confronting other people with their freedom. If we would shift the discussions of freedom from worrying about boundaries to worrying about how to maximize local choice and flexibility, we would evoke leadership instead of searching for it. Our beginning assumption would be that people are capable of using their freedom in service of the institution, and we would not put so much energy into setting hurdles that require people to demonstrate their worthiness to act freely.

Leaders, in this context, would also accept the idea that employee expectations of leaders are unfulfillable and need to be confronted. Leaders do not exist to meet the expectations of followers. When people ask you, "What is my future? What do you have in mind for me?" the answer is, "Nothing comes to mind in the moment. I am interested in what you have in mind for yourself." When employees express their disappointment in you as a leader, simply say, "I understand. I have my own questions about myself." We confront people with their accountability when we respect their own capacities, this gives us the flexibility to say no to them. Or "I don't know!" Clearly, explicitly. Too often our lips say yes, and no is left to the expression in our eyes. This is called lip service.

There is a crucial task for people in charge. Institutional and civic leaders exist to know the business we are in or developing. Leaders offer from the breadth of their positions to see where the institution should be placed in its marketplace. We need a vision about where the enterprise should be headed, and what the economic landscape within which we exist is. These are fair requests of leaders. To know the market, the environment in which we operate, and what is good for the whole. This is because they can see the whole thing. We do not need a vision from leaders about how we should behave and what values we should embrace. Employees have a deep sense of values and can be as trusted to live them out as fully as any trust we want to invest in our leaders. At what point did integrity become a quality defined by organizational level?

If leaders want to walk their talk, work as a team, listen well, and send single, consistent messages to the world, let them do it for their own sake, not for the sake of low-power people. We are condescending to each other when we think that leaders carry a special and unique role-model burden of expressing the humanity of the institution. If we eliminate leader as cause and employee as effect, this will work to eliminate the class structure in our institutions and reduce the social distance between levels. The privilege systems that differentiate by level and class do not serve the institution well; they only serve to reinforce our fear of the commons and our belief in a special ruling class. Leadership in an environment of freedom and accountability stands for each person being a manager, a leader, all responsible for the well-being of the larger world. This is not an argument against structure; it is about the distribution of power.

Those in power do have the responsibility of using that power with some grace. They need to take the idea of liberty seriously and work to eliminate oppressive controls. This is mostly an exercise in restraint. We need to stop managing people's time, managing their expenditures, worrying about on-the-job Internet journeys and personal phone calls. Go light on supervision, maybe even get rid of the word. Who has super vision anyway? Most of us end up wearing glasses regardless of our institutional level.

Although this might all appear soft-headed, it is actually the opposite. It creates a culture where people are held somewhat brutally accountable for meeting their promises and commitments. When we expect people to act as freely choosing individuals, we take away their excuses, de-legitimize their ability to blame others, and we put light in places where they or we once hid. This would begin to give us a real world.

Take a break for a moment. Here are some more ideas in Peter's language.

Choice, reality, and will

We never act like machines, that is, automatically. We cannot be machines, even if we wish to be. This means that all conscious acts are in effect choices among alternatives. That there exists a choice means that we-could-have-acted-otherwise, so that when we exclaim "I really had no choice in the matter," we cannot be understood to mean literally what we say, that we were helpless. Translated by philosophical insight, the sentence means that we decided or chose to do as we in fact did, either because we were intimidated and acted out of fear or because of some other, perhaps more rational, grounds. This stance declares that all states of consciousness—including those we ordinarily call choices as well as those we like to term inevitable actions—discloses a core experience of free will.

Choice and the nature of helplessness

If every one of our acts is a choice and that choice is free, then whenever we act consciously and deliberately, we also experience at the core of our action the sense of free will. In spite of the widespread feeling of helplessness and the avoidance of accountability in the culture, all states of consciousness consist of alternatives among which we must choose. The mature and authentic individual is fully conscious of the fact that they must choose, since free choice in actions cannot be avoided; i.e., that is not one of the alternatives open to us. Although we are free to choose, we are not free to choose to choose. This weight of always choosing becomes unbearably heavy. So, ordinarily, only when anguish accompanies the consciousness of our ever-present free will do we actually name that a choice. But that is a mere linguistic idiosyncrasy.

We always make a deliberate and persistent effort to keep in mind that every act we perform is, indeed, in its foundation a free one. If we never forget this fact about our human existence, we shall never be loath to assume willingly, cheerfully, and effectively the responsibility that is ours to begin with. Success in life and fulfillment as a human being are intimately tied to the clear and constant consciousness of this principle.

This means all statements of helplessness, all claims that it was not my fault, are factually incorrect. Despite any claims that I may make about the presence of coercion, the force of circumstances, or the lack of choice, each of my acts could have been performed otherwise— or, as a final alternative, could have been omitted altogether. Of course, the alternatives themselves are not infinite, but there are always more than one. The statements "I could not help myself" and "I had no choice" have, if taken strictly, no experiential correlate. They are rather emotive expressions of a double free choice: choice A is to perform act A, and choice B is to suppress as far as possible the consciousness that act a is the result of choice A.

Every act is free

By saying "I had no choice" (and meaning it), we have chosen to betray our human nature. We have, in that sentence, freely chosen to resign from the human race and join the technocracy of machines or electronics. But even while making this dehumanizing decision, we have not really succeeded at all in shedding our humanity, for, after all, the decision to be like a machine is a free—that is, typically human—act; it is an act that neither animal nor machine nor chip can perform! Even the attitude or decision that there is "really" no choice discloses itself to be a major and a free decision about the kind of person that we are going to be. Once it is clear, however, that we are humans—in Sartre's famous words, that we are "condemned to be free"—we will give up our futile and self-destructive efforts to deny our very nature. On the contrary, we will accept our nature and face the problem of making our life meaningful with redoubtable resoluteness.

Often, what makes it difficult to realize that all acts are free choices is that frequently all the alternatives open are unpleasant and painful. To be free certainly does not mean that the alternatives of paradisiacal pleasure and bountiful bliss are invariably open to us. To identify free will with pleasure is naïve. To be free simply means that there are always alternatives among which we can choose, even if none of the alternatives are ones we are pleased with.

The locus of freedom

Let us be certain that we understand what in our human experience is free and what is not.

First, whenever we act, we choose among alternatives, and this is one of the stubborn characteristics of our human existence. Second, the precise alternatives open to us are not subject to our free will. The particular nature of the alternatives is simply one of the invariant and overpowering characteristics of the world around and within us. This is called the conditions. Fate. Destiny. Given these limitations, we must understand that we constantly choose, regardless of how we may deny it. The consequences of this knowledge—in the Socratic spirit of "know thyself" and "virtue is knowledge"—is emotional maturity.

Realizing the fact and nature of our freedom makes us mature; it gives us the reins of our life—we can exercise control, direction, and command over our own life. We each become, in short, an individual, with all the satisfaction, concreteness, solidity, and security that this implies. Successful and authentic living and action requires a constant consciousness of the fullness of our freedom and the corresponding responsibility and control.

Accepting responsibility and accountability

The willingness to accept full responsibility—that is, to be accountable for all the implications of our actions—grows directly out of accepting the fact of our free will. Once the inevitability of accountability is recognized, we will be inclined to place the full blame on ourselves rather than on others or on objective situations beyond our control. Once we are clear about the fact that, whether we like or approve, we are fully accountable for the general character of our lives, for our actions and omissions, only then will we resolutely take the stance that we are willing to assume these responsibilities. When we see the inevitability of a demand, we can willingly engage in its execution. This is not about guilt. It is the dimension of owning our experience and how we touch the world around us.

Adapted from Peter Koestenbaum, "The Power of Freedom," in *The Vitality of Death: Essays in Existential Psychology and Philosophy,* Westport, CT: Greenwood Publishing Co., 1971. Originally reprinted with permission from *International Forum for Existential Psychiatry* 1, no. 2 (Summer 1966): 208–218 and 1, no. 3 (Fall 1966): 323–337.

2 | The Potential of Anxiety

As individuals, we spend enormous energy defending against anxiety, and this is reflected in our organizational life. We try to construct a workplace where anxiety is reduced to a manageable distraction. The common managerial injunction, "Don't bring me problems, bring me solutions," is a good example of our defense against the ambiguity and uncertainty of life.

> " . . . there is a cost to our freedom, and that is the anxiety that accompanies it. We need to change our mind about anxiety and learn to embrace it. We reclaim our freedom when we come to terms with the anxiety that is associated with it."
> — Peter Koestenbaum (1978)

Much of what we usually describe as bureaucracy—caution, slavishness to rules, needing many approvals before doing anything—is really a defense against our individual and collective anxiety. We usually don't attribute our caution to our own experience of anxiety; we are more likely to attribute cause to our bosses or to our subordinates, or to anyone who happens to be in our field of vision at the moment.

This pervasive point of view—that my anxiety, along with many other emotions, is caused by the external world—is placed in question by the philosophy we are writing about. This view outlines the revealing and transforming potential of anxiety and opens the possibility that this experience of tension that I have been running from, and that organizations are organized to deny, needs to be embraced, welcomed, and accepted.

"Philosophers make an important and well-known distinction between existential and neurotic anxiety. Neurotic anxiety is not a separate type but rather a dysfunctional derivative of the basic anxiety, which is existential. Existential anxiety is healthy and is the natural condition of the person when in a state of self-disclosure. Neurotic anxiety is diseased and is the denial of existential anxiety. . . . In other words, neurotic anxiety is a function of existential anxiety. The function is denial. [It is the fear of how others and the world see you. It is the basic fear of being a fool.] The basis is existential anxiety. This distinction is important because it reverses the conventional view that all anxiety is pathological. We no longer need to be surprised that our attempts to 'cure' anxiety do not work!"

— *Peter Koestenbaum (1978)*

The implications of this point of view are enormous. If we could learn to live with anxiety and see it as a positive key to our own well-being, and not something erasable or caused by others, we could then drop our defensive routines. Drop the narrative that does not work that well anyway. We could begin to trust ourselves more and to trust each other. We would be less fearful of people in power, for we would realize that the grief we thought they brought us was in reality unavoidably self-inflicted.

"When anxiety is denied, our nature is denied. . . . As a result, the price we pay for the denial of existential anxiety is severe. The dominant consequence is to restrict our life."

— *Peter Koestenbaum (1978)*

The fruits of your patience

A friendly caution. You may grow weary of all this talk of anxiety and of having to absorb concepts such as consciousness that come with definitions that slip away one minute after they have been articulated.

It is also possible you may at times become impatient with continually dwelling on subjects that seem to hold a negative cast and language that often confuses more than clarifies. The common response to philosophy—at least for most of us—is to drift and lose some interest. This response, in itself, is interesting for it is likely a measure of how embedded we are in rationality and science and psychology as a way of explaining our experience. There is no language that the larger culture has less patience with than the language of philosophy.

"The 'normal' condition is to have much of the philosophic truth about us permanently repressed. The more this truth can be tolerated, the more authentic is the individual. Many individuals can tolerate little and would rather die than see it. Part of the problem is social bias against the seeing the world as it is. Ignorance of philosophy leads people to recoil in terror when philosophic truth becomes revealed."
— *Peter Koestenbaum (1978)*

The first response to philosophic thinking and language is to want to get practical. "How does this apply to how I operate in the real world?" "Give a proof of concept." "Why can't you use words that I am familiar with?"

This impatience, while fair game and valid, is also an example of the theory presented here, for the impatience is an example of the experience itself—it is our anxiety. And we want to solve it. We want to transform anxiety—an experience, a feeling, a reaction—into some action that will make it go away. And so we want proof.

Our institutions use the need for speed and time and convenience as the argument for action. We feel that reflection, introspection, and inward thought take too long. If something cannot be done quickly, it is not worth doing—there is something wrong with it. This is true at every level, whether it is the hunt for quarterly earnings improvement, the need to shorten the cycle time of a new product or process, the desired training time for new skills, or the search for a living God. We value speed over depth and action over insight.

> "[W]e human beings—because of our tendency to conceptualize our experience in terms of external-objects alone rather than in terms of a first person, I-am-the-subject-that-is-the-object field. . .—fear our own nature. We deny the truth about ourselves, and we deny our source of insight. We try to kill the anxiety that is in reality the messenger of the gods."
>
> — Peter Koestenbaum (1978)

While of course there is a marketplace requirement for timeliness and we know there are just so many hours in the day, our desire for speed and concreteness is more than a rational response to environmental requirements. It has invaded every aspect of our lives. I can't watch television without a remote control; I need quick service on vacation; I even want to know the sex of my unborn child. And I want my meals delivered prepared and on time.

Solving anxiety

All of these qualities of modern culture can be viewed as a way of life in the Digital Age, but they can also be seen as symptoms of how isolated we are as we manage our own anxiety, which is to escape it or eliminate it. It is a part of our desire for belonging. For much of my life, in fact until I ran into Peter and his philosophy, I viewed anxiety as a weakness, a problem to be solved. I was anxious about being anxious. One place this became so visible was when I had to make a presentation for my work.

As with many of us, the prospect of public speaking created great stress. I would worry about the talk, I would over or under prepare, I would produce too many PowerPoint slides, and even then, in some dark moments, I would imagine my escape. I would wonder what would happen if I did not even show up for the presentation. How far could I get before I would have to pay a price for my irresponsibility?

At one level you might say that what I needed was more confidence, more practice perhaps, some training in public speaking, or some private affirmations I could speak to shore myself up. While all of this might help some, these actions represent a solution to a wrongly defined problem. The presentation was not the problem.

The problem was my response to the experience of being afraid or anxious—what existential philosophy would call my neurotic anxiety. What I did not realize for too long was that the tension I felt about speaking to groups was a sign of life. It was choosing moments that evoked anxiety that was dragging me more actively into finding my own voice, owning my wish to present a perfect face to the world, helping me find my own legs to stand on.

"When we are anxious, we experience the truth. But when we are anxious about being anxious, we are sick and needlessly limit our potential for enjoying life—and we do not experience the truth."
— *Peter Koestenbaum (1978)*

At some point, though, the physical experience of the anxiety was attractive. I began to see it as water into which I needed to dive—realizing that the anxiety was an invitation to move toward those things I had tried to avoid. This revelation shifted my response to the fear, and I actually got pretty good at speaking to groups. I still do not really enjoy it, but it gives meaning to the ideas that I care about and gives me a platform from which I can engage the world. Most of us, in the face of anxiety, think we need to relocate. New job. New relationships. Go back to school. More yoga. Better eating. Better medication. A New Year's resolution. All consumerist assumptions looking for a cure. Believing that anxiety is a problem to be solved. I wish.

The promise of anxiety

This instinct to treat anxiety as the enemy drives a great deal of our behavior at work, in the so-called real world. The workplace raises for each of us a bundle of anxious emotions. We worry about our bosses and how they feel about us. We carry the burden of promises we made that we may not deliver on; we are embroiled in territorial disputes, and budget pressure, and on it goes. And then pandemic comes, and the bundle of challenges at work now explode at home.

We spend enormous time and energy trying to solve these pressures by applying more structure and definition. We fill out feedback forms on our bosses. We develop complex project management protocols for our promises. There are staff groups with no power called Performance Management. We meet endlessly, trying to define and negotiate territory. We spend endless resources on information technology, in the belief that if we watch money more closely, pray to big data, it will solve our uncertainty and be the key to being productive.

The insight of philosophy gives us a chance to see all these responses to our anxiety as simply attempts to eliminate or solve what are inherent qualities of being a human being and part of a human organization. This insight has the potential to save us time and resources if we could reframe the question and stop trying to fix what in reality is not a problem but a signpost that something important is on the table. Anxiety is designed and built into the experience of being part of an organization, especially one that survives by delivering results. The moment we shift our thinking about our experience, in the ways Peter writes about, then new possibilities open up for our institutions.

> *"If we do not feel anxious it may be appropriate to encourage it for the sake of rebirth. For our learning or transformation to be effective and truly reconstructive we must seek out the maximum amount of tolerable anxiety. The changes that occur in intensive transformational experiences do so by undermining our deepest suppressed assumptions—a condition of grave anxiety. Such anxiety must be encouraged for rebirth to take place. We can mobilize the anxiety of*

birth, and thus facilitate growth, when we are given first of all—by life events, or another person—a 'shocking' assessment of ourselves. . . . The shock must be strong enough to undermine the old and nonworking world design of ourselves, but not so violent as to arouse more anxiety than we are able to cope with."

— *Peter Koestenbaum (1978)*

The language of freedom: It was an inside job

There is a fine line between philosophy, religion, and spirituality. They all occupy the domain of feeling, experience, and consciousness, which balance our more common focus on data, reason, and science. The language of philosophy, religion, and spirituality—while it is about real life and is based on the fact of who we are—is more like poetry than engineering speech in that it seeks those areas of life that are paradoxical and defy clear measurement.

"[W]e must understand and facilitate the transition of our age from one of technology to one of inner-space exploration. We must, together, invent the new symbols and meanings for the age that wishes to be born. We must allow ourselves to be the prophets through which our culture invents these symbols. . . . This is not a time to lose faith in our future, nor is it a time to lose our nerve."

— *Peter Koestenbaum (1978)*

The language of philosophy is poetic and complex by design, for language is a primary way that we express our freedom and, in a sense, acknowledge it into existence. Language is the delivery system of transformation. Not talk. Language. Narrative. Linguistics.

The common language of the culture in place, sometimes called the default or dominant culture, is anything but poetic. It is primarily the language of engineering and economics and marketing and some psychology. In our organizations, we use the language of results, outcomes, negotiation, and barter. We talk of systems, strategy, and appraisal. Schedules, metrics, and milestones. Data and information management. Competency models, modifying and prescribing desired behavior. The bottom line and the ones above it become the point. This is inherited story line, which is that the core of our culture grows from the language of the free-market consumer culture.

The language of freedom is quite different. Even the word *freedom* seems traditionally out of place in institutions. But if we want to come to terms with our freedom, and the accountability that comes with it, then we are taken into the language of the poet, prophet, or songwriter. Priests are also in the mix. The language akin to deepening our experience uses words like *forgiveness, destiny, confession, compassion, wisdom, feeling, guilt, ambivalence, transformation, revelation*. And *accountability*. Which all are the antithesis of certainty.

These words not only describe the world of the soul and all that is human, but they in fact create it. If we want our organizations to become more humanly habitable, more supportive of developing the capacity of the person, more able to manage the uncertainty of a pandemic and postpandemic world, and also more focused on purpose first, economics second, then it begins with a shift in language. The language is one of the challenges of a book on philosophy, for purposely using language that defies definition becomes a political point. The language we use declares where the power lies.

Will we decide to take the language of philosophy, and perhaps what it means to be human, and force fit it into the mindset of engineering and economics? Or do we bring the unadulterated language of our humanity and soul into the world of work, and thereby occupy some of the space formerly held exclusively by rationality and scientific proof? The final answer will be that we need both ways of constructing the world, which is why we included the idea of chosen accountability in the explorations here. It is a declaration that we need both the economist and the philosopher defining the nature of our institutions. It is a mistake, however, to smooth over the political significance of the words we use by getting too chummy with them too quickly.

It is because words like *revelation, guilt, forgiveness,* and *compassion* seem somewhat out of place in many (not all) institutions, that the use of these words is powerful. At stake is the answer to the question of who defines reality—the economist or the philosopher or you? Top management or ourselves and our peers? In Western culture, the economist has had full rein in defining what counts and deciding how we measure how we are doing. This began with the act of enclosure in 1600s England. The moment when public land could sustain all but was privatized for the profitability of a fenced-in sheep pasture. Our materialistic, consumer-driven society is a baby step from that moment.

Shifting the context to freedom and accountability

The fact that we are increasingly interested in the subjects of freedom, meaning, and destiny, though, means that something's blowing in the wind and has been for some time. For several years now, books on purpose, poetry, and spirituality have sold well into the organization marketplace. These books and ideas, however publicly growing, have stayed on the periphery; they have been used more as coping strategies to make outcome- and control-driven organizations more tolerable. What has not happened, though, is any real shift in the basic context of our organizations, which would be to believe that philosophic insights are essential to the survival of an institution, and its connection to the marketplace, and provide a basis for governance.

The reason for shifting the context from economics to philosophy is to create a culture of accountability. We have been in a period where accountability is under assault. Entitlement is strong, and people feel less responsible for the whole. We act as if the question "What's in it for me?" is a reasonable and useful one. And working at home is going to stick around. We are free agents, and loyalty to any one organization is becoming more elastic. In communities, we live in the isolation of our cell phones, video and social media, and backyard. We treat government and public education as if our neighborhood and raising our children could be outsourced.

The focus here on an existential view of human freedom and human destiny demands a level of personal accountability that our institutions and culture had not contemplated. Maybe by Steve Jobs in his garage. And now with the preference and opportunity to work at home most of the time, if we continue to have to hold people accountable, then we will continue to focus on compliance and miss the value of accountability that is chosen. Our language is the starting point to discover accountability that is chosen as a consequence of claiming our freedom.

> *"At these moments, we discover how grossly we have neglected our freedom, how we have neglected taking charge of our life. Our whole existence reflects the absence of our freedom. Through the anxiety of birth, we can see in one flash how life can be reorganized in its very foundations. We often discover that throughout our life we have allowed external circumstances, publicly broadcasted values, and accidental relationships to determine what is to be of meaning in our existence. We suddenly realize the philosophic fact that we do have an inner foundation, an internal resource, and that this ground is of far greater importance than whatever our social environment could possibly offer."*
>
> — *Peter Koestenbaum (1978)*

Implications: Anxiety as an ally of accountability both central to performance in a time of permanent uncertainty

A move toward freedom-based institutions asks us to rethink how we embrace anxiety at work. Whether work is home or office or Main Street. As we have said, organizations spend great energy defending against anxiety. As if anxiety and productivity are in opposition to each other. This is despite our experience of being anxious whenever we are under pressure to perform. Our earliest institutional experience was attending school, having to compete against our peers, and it is hard to remember taking a test that did not make us anxious. What made this early performance pressure doubly difficult was not only the anxiety, but the feeling that we should not be anxious. It does not have to be so, for part of what characterizes high performers is their ability to accept anxiety, to use it as a source of motivation and energy.

> *"To run in anguish from anxiety is futile, since anxiety will not go away any more than our breath will go away. To be 'cured' of anxiety makes as much sense as to be 'cured' of heartbeats or of metabolism. Once we have accepted anxiety as right and proper, we can begin to build creatively on the experience."*
> — *Peter Koestenbaum (1978)*

Our action plan here is to treat anxiety as a friend, understanding it as a form of excitement and a sign that we are alive and in fact living our lives. It also, when accepted, creates places of belonging. We are most alive when we have a sense of purpose, and we only know this when there is tension about the outcome and the recognition that something is on the line. It is difficult to imagine finding meaning in a purpose where nothing is at stake.

If work is one of the primary places where purpose is pursued and results are required, then anxiety and its cousin, surprise, are the signs that we have shown up and taken it all to heart. With this in mind, here are some of the forms of our struggle with anxiety in our institutions.

A problem to be solved

Most organized efforts, therapy included, big pharma included, treat anxiety as a problem to be solved. The common statement by managers, "Don't bring me a problem, bring me a solution," is a pure play against our uncertainty and the complexity of the world. It is the illusory stance that all problems have solutions, and we can find them if we just try harder. Even if our past attempts at solutions have not worked. This is another version of the triumph of science over religion. The broader expression of this is that we believe that if employees are anxious about some aspect of the uncertain future, managers need to reassure this anxiety, as if employee anxiety is a management problem. Plus, if you ever are in a position of giving feedback to a leader, the most common response is, "Well, I am not surprised." As if a disaster is more welcome than not knowing.

When we take freedom seriously, we treat anxiety as a sign that the system is alive. Say we are anxious about the progress of a project that is vulnerable, or about what will happen to our unit, or that top management is about to visit and look us over. The fact that these are sources of anxiety means that people care about what is happening. This creates an opportunity for us—individual and organization—to become clearer about our purpose and to affirm the choice we are making to be in this organization.

"[A]nxiety is the experience of creativity. All creative acts—artistic, loving, scholarly, scientific, political, social, and so forth—are born of anxiety and made possible through anxiety. All great creative people have translated the experience of anxiety into the act and product of creation."

— *Peter Koestenbaum (1978)*

Instead of a time for reassuring people that things will work out and that employees should trust management, uncertainty and anxiety create an opportunity for a different kind of dialogue. Doubts and fears can be expressed, acknowledged, recognized as real and not immediately soluble. This can lead to a serious discussion of the choice how people want to be together in this organization. The question for employees is to have them consider the choice in front of them and to see that the threat gives them an opportunity to be more fully in charge of their own lives and of the way they decide to be in the middle of this business. No cheerleading needed. There may be a silver lining in those clouds, but they are still clouds.

Lists and measures

Our compulsion for lists and structured measures is the essence of our response to anxiety, going under the name of an unpredictable future. It is not that lists and measures are not important. It is just they are not the point. The common practice of ending every training session and every meeting with a summary list of things to do is an effort to carve some reassurance that our being together in the meeting had some value. No sin to make a list, but the really important things we need to do or remember, we hold onto without a reminder system.

If we treated anxiety as a friend, we might notice what situations generate our anxiety and ask ourselves whether it is the situation itself or our response to the situation that troubles us. We tend to measure and watch each other more closely when our faith in ourselves and others falters. Instead of controlling more tightly through measurement and milestone practices, we might ask what deeper and more personal concerns might be driving our low confidence.

Some of our anxiety comes under the heading of neurotic guilt. Neurotic guilt comes from having betrayed ourselves. Instead of claiming our freedom, we have given it away. At work, self-betrayal comes in the form of saying yes when we mean no. We make promises that we cannot really commit to or believe in. We agree to goals that are rarely achieved. Or quotas that are handed to us. We say everything is all right when it is not.

"Anxiety has a tendency to rise when in the presence of [what is challenging and unpredictable]. This is true in our experiences at home and in our communities, and often most dramatically at work. Another way to say this is that anxiety is highly contagious. . . . Existential anxiety is contagious because insight is communicable— even without putting it into words through declarative, abstract, language, [when we witness people claiming their choice, it infects us]. Neurotic anxiety—because it cripples existential anxiety and

distorts the possibilities of existential anxiety—is also contagious.
Its residue is transmitted in human interactions [which produce
isolation]."

— *Peter Koestenbaum (1978)*

We hold the myth that you can't say no. Our institutional
anxiety about freedom gets expressed in our fear of refusal.
We are afraid of disobedience, and as a result, in most
organizations there is an injunction against saying no. The
common phrase "if you stand up you get shot" is our belief
that saying no, or saying yes too loudly, is tantamount to an act
of terrorism or mutiny, an assault against authority that is
dangerous to the institution. It is interesting that self-
management used to be called mutiny, which was considered
an act of treason. We are all inundated in the need to be a
"team player," which, in its use in our organizations, is an
argument about the dangers of freedom.

"One of the most difficult problems in being a manager or leader—or
in having some power over others, which includes consultants and
other helpers and healers—is dealing with the anxiety of those
around us. And the hardest part in this is the fact that anxiety in
the subordinates, clients, bosses, or others arouses our own anxiety."

— *Peter Koestenbaum (1978)*

All of this is part of the elusive complexity of our struggle
with our freedom and subsequent accountability. We want a
safe path, and we want management to provide it. What we
want is to say no or to withhold a promise and not have to
pay a price for it. Heavy dependence on lists, action plans, and
milestones is our effort to hedge against paying for our

ambivalence about really deciding what to commit to at work. If we viewed our anxiety as inherent in being human, and knew that we cannot drive it away, we could stop trying so hard to manage and control it and eliminate some of the excessive hunger for numbers, measures, and other modes of prediction. We would value surprise, which is another word for doubt and not knowing.

Our wish for certainty

We also defend against anxiety in the way we spend time strategizing how to relate to one another, especially if we are trying to influence each other. I have attended many meetings where the business was deciding how to handle the next meeting or how to influence top management on some change effort. We have communications departments to manage the words of exchange. The political nature of organizations is reinforced by the need to be strategic in our relationships. We think that if we can control or predict how a conversation will go, it will improve its quality and get us what we want. This penchant for planning our encounters is a distrust of ourselves and each other as spontaneous beings.

The need to plan who we want to be is especially true when leaders speak to their employees or in public. Town hall meetings. Communication experts position leader remarks; we have PowerPoints to maintain focus; and we meet in auditoriums that keep our leaders physically above and apart from their own people. And sometimes we even ask the audience to pass in their questions ahead of time so we can screen them and prepare our responses. In pandemic times, same process, just on camera.

All of this shows a distrust of real, spontaneous, free conversation—held in real time. It is a distrust of our leaders to be powerful and caring and relevant without a script. It is a belief that the world has to be managed, and that employees and citizens want their leaders to be rehearsed, positioned, turned into models of competence. When did we begin to call this the real world? It is an impressions-marketing world. It is as imprisoning to the leaders as much as it is an effort to manage employee attitudes and motivation. And allowing time for questions and answers is more of the same. Employees have the questions and executives have the answers.

Covid has simply magnified the permanent uncertainty of the world. Trying to solve anxiety by offering manufactured certainty as medicine and allowing our fear of spontaneity shape our way of connecting with each other. These all interfere with experiencing our freedom and reducing accountability in all the players in our organizations. They also increase our isolation, reduce our sense of belonging. We have a difficult time accepting that the existence of anxiety is proof that organizations are living systems. When we accept the fact of our freedom, it carries with it a willingness to acknowledge anxiety as a permanent condition, not a problem to be solved. This is the runway toward chosen accountability.

The permanent condition

If we choose to acknowledge that our freedom is at the heart of high performance and creating a better future and come to value anxiety and accountability as aspects of the air that we breathe, we would:

1. **See anxiety as a friend.** Seek it out as a clue or doorway to deeper meaning, which can be found in the practical, day-to-day aspects of institutional life. We would find anxiety interesting and worth understanding instead of something to be eliminated. When people ask questions that have no clear answers, we simply say, "I don't know."

2. **Stop protecting people from bad news,** from our uncertainty about what we plan to do, and from our own leadership doubts. We would trust that others had the maturity to accept leaders as whole and incomplete human beings. We would recognize that each of us has the strength or can develop the strength to face the harsh reality of life and work. It does not serve any of us to be protected against the truth. Our employees and associates are not children, they just often act that way.

3. **Judge our meetings and gatherings on how clearly our anxiety gets expressed.** When asked, "How was the meeting?" we would stop thinking the meeting was good because everyone was comfortable, optimistic, and supportive. We would believe that the meeting was good because concerns, doubts, and feelings were fully expressed. When we know how we all feel and where we all stand, we have a real sense of the real world.

4. **Keep in perspective all the effort to clearly define roles, to prescribe competencies, and to live according to plan.** These practices are most useful for the conversation and understanding they evoke rather than the document they produce. To function according to role, to train according to competencies, and to assess the world according to plan are escapes from the uncertainty that our freedom precipitates. Adhered to closely, they become a means of control which is, once again, a defense against anxiety and tend to constrain our performance and creativity rather than release it. Sorry for the repetition, but I am a participant in all I am describing.

5. **Stop oversight.** Very common in the community world as well as the business world. We consistently respond to anxiety by trying to create a world that appears more certain than it actually is and that needs more control and supervision than it actually does. Planning and structure are, of course, useful things, as long as they are not mistaken for being our purpose or the point. Organizations spend more resources and time in oversight and trying to predict the future than the return on these efforts warrants. We believe that people or teams will perform better and more honestly when they are watched. We have accepted the need for oversight and control, even though there is little evidence that more oversight and control lead to higher performance. No one measures the cost of oversight, and there is some evidence that high-control systems are actually low performing in quickly changing environments.

6. **Value spontaneity and vulnerability in dialogue.** Replace presentations with conversation. Four to four hundred in circles. Virtual meetings primarily in groups

for five. Choose an unscripted existence, realizing that the mistakes we make are an expression of our humanity and spontaneity and sources of organizational and personal learning. We then leave room for dissent and value it. We stop seeing questions and serious disagreement as having anything to do with team playing.

This all leads to the insight that many of our performance management systems are really designed to increase our comfort level more than our performance level. Uncertainty and its uneasiness is an inherent quality of a human system and a device to force us to exercise choice. Knowing that, we begin to discover ways to create cultures of accountability.

Being conscious

Each of us spins our past like a cobweb. We see what our empty consciousness has created by looking at our past. But we no longer are that past—we only were it. We are now and always a present-creating-its-past. Thus, the experiences of ambition and accomplishment are values associated with the process of creating the past. Consequently, anxiety informs us of the meaning of life because anxiety is that meaning. To be anxious is the meaning. Anxiety discloses our substantiality to us. It tells us how to go about creating ourselves in the future, distinct from the story of our past is what fuels the content of the meaning of life.

Second, uncertainty is the motivation to meaning. A life without anxiety is static, like a rock. Anxiety introduces disequilibrium; it creates an imbalance which develops a goal of resoluteness. The search for meaning is brought about through the phenomenon of anxiety.

A third value of anxiety is that it arouses us to the significance of love and compassion; it alerts us to the incontrovertible need for care and concern. Anxiety proves to us the value of tenderness. The emptiness of anxiety, its sense of isolation, separation, and abandonment, urgently points to the axiomatic need for closeness, oneness, and intimacy. What is there to share if it is not one's anxiety?

Fourth, anxiety is also the experience of time, and with it, of futurity and hope. Anxiety discloses our structure as intentional beings; it therefore purifies for us the experience of time that we are. And being time, we are also that toward which time moves, which is the future. And in disclosing to us our futurization, anxiety is the experience of hope.

Finally, anxiety is the experience of creativity. All creative acts— artistic, loving, scholarly, scientific, political, social, and so forth—are born of anxiety and made possible through anxiety. All great creative people have translated the experience of anxiety into the act of creation. Time and creativity together fashion growth. Anxiety is thus essential to growth. In fact, the experience of anxiety is the experience of growth.

Adapted from Peter Koestenbaum, *The New Image of the Person: The Theory and Practice of Clinical Philosophy,* Westport, CT: Greenwood Publishing Co., 1978.

3

Speaking of Death and Evil

One of the consistent gifts of philosophy is its capacity to take us deeper, to help us spiral inward into rooms of our experience that are a little dusty from lack of use. This section takes us into the redemptive quality of facing strong words and ideas like evil and death. They come to us in symbolic ways such as failures, which are little deaths, and disappointments, which are a reminder that there are things in the world that we cannot control. Evil can take the form of manipulation and saying something other than what we mean. To take advantage of others' vulnerability just because we can. Most often we turn away from death and evil, hoping it will be postponed or disappear. Here we look more deeply into them, offering the possibility that becoming better acquainted with the darker, shadow side of life is another essential element of our transformation and freedom. Facing evil and death as they occur is actually a way to find choice in the moments when they appear. Thanks to Carl Jung.

"It is increasingly common in our efforts at personal growth—resulting perhaps from Freud's discovery of aggression as fundamental and Jung's discovery of the pervasive presence of what he called the shadow—to learn to accept our dark side, to accept negative emotions as natural."

— *Peter Koestenbaum (1971)*

Early in my relationship with this philosophy, I began to get the point that all the territory I had avoided was exactly the ground on which I needed to tread. Peter had an image that held great meaning for me: "When you are drowning, dive." When I most wanted to surface and avoid the heaviness of loss, failure, and even philosophy, this was just the time to go more deeply into it. The phrase comes from being caught in the undertow on a beach. When the current tries to pull you out to sea, you will exhaust yourself if you try to swim against it. If, on the other hand, you surrender to it and let it take you out to sea, it will gently deposit you a few hundred yards offshore, in waters calm enough that you can swim back to shore.

"Our freedom is capable of withstanding evil—of saying no to it. Our freedom is our only opportunity to choose to be noble, to stand up to evil, to counteract evil."

— Peter Koestenbaum (1971)

The title of Peter's book *The Vitality of Death* is, in itself, a clue to where we step. How could death be presented with such optimism, as something vital rather than discouraging? Death is not a pleasant subject. Nor a subject you often find in a book about leadership and organizational life. In fact, it is something we seem determined to avoid, especially in American culture, which romanticizes youth, expects us to live forever, and even treats dying as a medical, technological, or smoking, drinking, or dietary failure. We are burdened with stories of immortality in the form of a ninety-year-old soul skydiving with fearless enthusiasm.

"Death is a fact of life—that is a universal truth. The recognition of the nature of the anticipation of death has rejuvenating and revitalizing effects on human existence. That is another fact of life. What the decision is, or should be, about the meaning of life is, perhaps unfortunately, a burdensome individual decision. But the decision will come—since we often know what we really want—as soon as the urgency of reaching a conclusion is brought home to us through the fact of inexorable death."

— Peter Koestenbaum (1971)

Death is an option

The discussion of death confronts me with the fact that I will not live forever. Not exactly headline news. Institutions have a hard time with endings. They act is if they will live forever. It is the arrogance of immortality. We seem to be habitually compelled to sustain optimism, even in the face of contrary data. What we face in the workplace is the possibility of symbolic death—in other words, failure. Or no growth. Or a declining stock price or budget. We cling to the illusory notion that failure is not an option. Witness the popular notion that innovation is best achieved by the idea of "fail fast." Get it over with. The positive is to see failing as a learning strategy. When we deny failure as useful, we continue to invest in projects that are not working, partly because we confuse failure with defeat. Just because something we tried does not work, it doesn't mean we were wrong to begin it, or that there is something wrong with us. In fact, we constantly deal with failure, especially when the unpredictability of the world demands that we choose adventure when all we wanted was safety.

We have a long tradition in science that understands that discovery and creativity require us to change our minds about failure. One of the gifts of the scientific method is that it teaches us that failure is as valuable as success, that discovery comes from being surprised, and that if we desire to grow, we need to embrace accidents, moments of unpredictability, as a learning opportunity rather than treating them as a source of shame.

"We are in fact responsible for success as well as for failure in life, irrespective of whether we are prepared to accept and assume such responsibility."

— *Peter Koestenbaum (1971)*

Also, and most compelling, is the chaos and unpredictability that surround us. No organization is a secure place anymore; our structures, relationships, how we do what we do are in a fast and constant state of flux. The pandemic was a dramatic and painful expression of this. So the workplace that might have been a refuge of security is now a source of unpredictability. Even the large and great organizations are standing on shaky ground. Who would have imagined that it is a question of valued employees choosing to come to the office only once in a while? Or thirty-four million people quitting their jobs? They might return, but the leaving was a shot across the bow.

The typical way we deal with failure and chaos is to problem solve and create programs. Initiate reform efforts. They are about better leadership, cultural change efforts to foster creativity, holding people accountable. Higher, performance-based pay. At times we see failure as a disruption and a good thing. Mostly we celebrate the disruption of businesses other than our own. We reassure ourselves that chaos is a step in the journey, that just around the corner, the chaos will stop vibrating, and nature will provide us with the order that we seek. In a pandemic era, we looked for the new normal. The old normal, however, wasn't really that normal. We had just become used to it. All of these are versions of experiencing small versions of the end of something, death in a smaller form.

The philosopher brings to us the intimate relationship between living a full, meaningful life and our willingness to look death squarely in the eye. Our fears, our failures, our experience of being assaulted and destabilized by change, in fact, can only be genuinely dealt with by experientially accepting the fact we are going to die—what Peter terms the *death of myself.* In essence he says that we are most likely to fail, be controlled by our fears, and be toppled by change if we do not face the question of death directly.

> *"The fact that failure and death are used in ordinary language as if they had one and the same meaning blurs death in its two meanings—death of myself and death of another. This is of fundamental importance."*
> — Peter Koestenbaum (1971)

A storm in the shelter

This question of death, in the form of failure, more than any other, has represented a dividing line between the philosopher and the person of practical action. We have asked those who lead us to shelter us from the prospect of something, including us, dying. We demand optimism from them, we insist they convince us that what might have seemed like a mistake, or what Peter would term a symbolic death, was really just a stage in strategic realignment. Fail fast.

I remember when the Coca-Cola Company brought out New Coke with great fanfare. It was a cornerstone of how Coca-Cola would stay ahead of its competition. Six months into the promotion, it became obvious that the marketplace did not want a new Coke; they wanted the old one. The company had underestimated the loyalty customers had for the original taste and brand. This was an existential crisis for those who worked for the company. They had never experienced failure on such a public scale. Some kept believing that bringing out a product that the public did not embrace was really a clever strategic ploy, for it created great publicity, and reinforced the sales of the old product, which they called Classic Coke.

I saw employees at times looking up at the Coca-Cola headquarters tower in Atlanta as if faith in a superior being had been stolen from them. It was a very difficult emotional time for all Coca-Cola employees. Interestingly, at one point the company gave most salaried employees a check for $100 just to let people know that management knew how much heat they were taking from their friends about the New Coke. Interesting example of how organizations deal with their shame. And a mistake. It is a denial of failure, a small death, in soft drinks after all, but a wound on a collective psyche.

If we wish to seriously deal with fear and failure, then death—its symbolic meaning and our relationship to it—needs to be present in our thinking. Our discussion of death serves us in understanding and reframing how we think about failure and gives us a means, grounded in human experience and not in rhetoric, to create productive and meaningful institutions and leaders.

> "[I]f we ask, 'How much life have I left?' the answer is we do not know how much of our life remains—maybe less than a year, maybe a year, maybe a great deal more. Some of that, of course,

*depends on us, on our physical and mental health habits. But most
is out of our hands. Our generic problems are, in the last analysis,
the same that confront us in the hypothetical example of being told
that we have but one year to live. Authentic success, decision, genuine
happiness, full meaning, these goals can be achieved only in light of
the clear insight into the fact that all of us have been condemned to die."*
— *Peter Koestenbaum (1971)*

Facing reality. Taking charge of our life.

Facing the reality that we are not immortal, that some of our
plans do not work, and that our institutions are not everlasting
forces us to be more truthful about our predicament. If we
want our organizations to really be the real world, we need to
give voice to the reality of whatever our current condition is.
Too often positioning replaces telling the truth. Public
relations becomes a strategy of deflection and positivism.

> *"The vitality of death lies in that it makes almost impossible the
> repression of unpleasant but important realities. We do not accept
> any excuses to postpone dealing with our basic problems nor to hide
> these from ourselves. The realization of death carries with it the
> successful management of many unconscious and repressed problems.
> One who is about to die does not practice the art of self-deception.
> Death makes us honest."*
> — *Peter Koestenbaum (1971)*

The argument for positioning and not telling the truth is
that people do not want to hear the truth. And that it slips
into a marketing challenge. Our audience is not only the
consumer public, but our own employees. Managers believe

that their job is to protect their employees from upsetting news; they try to shelter their people from anxiety and harm. This kind of parenting only demeans employees in their capacity to handle the world as it is. If we want employees to be accountable for the well-being of the institution, they need to be a part of its struggles and live with its vulnerability— even with the possibility that the institution might not survive, or that it does make mistakes, and this is an early warning system that we can no longer continue in its present form.

The strength that is built by looking squarely at the harsh reality facing us, the ultimate harsh reality being that this path is my end and we will eventually die, is the strongest way to face our anxiety. When we see that our organization is not as strong as we hoped it might be, we then have the information to choose to be accountable for its well-being, regardless of what tomorrow might bring.

The exploration of death here also underscores that each of our lives carries within it the drama that we might have thought was reserved for public figures or artists who were forced to confront, because of their position or their talent, great issues of life and death. It does not take wartime or the threat of great loss or a pandemic to justify our concerns about questions of courage and death and greater purpose. We each are central figures in the world; we each were given gifts that place an obligation on us. So these questions become urgent to us, regardless of the history or the story that might have brought us to this point.

"To accept death means to take charge of one's life. One who sees the genuine function of death in life is no fatalist. They do not feel strictured. On the contrary, they are the freest of all. Nothing holds them back but their own free decisions. There is nothing to fear, nothing to be timid about, no reason to feel dependent, inadequate, or inferior; for we have once and for all conquered the ultimate threat."

— *Peter Koestenbaum (1978)*

A summary of usefulness of the reality of death

We discover the vitality of death, the positive and beneficial aspects of the fact of death, by deepening our understanding of these philosophic insights:

1. *We cannot escape death—real or symbolic or small in the moment. We must construct our life—daily actions as well as major, overall plans—with the full and clear realization of that fact. We must accept, once and for all and without any reservation, misgiving, false hope, repression, or bitterness, the fact that we have been condemned to this early warning system for death. Then we can become alive. In accepting, we will neutralize an otherwise completely demoralizing and paralyzing fear. This is one key to the successful navigation of human existence.*

2. *Once we have recognized and admitted the inevitability of our death, then we are on the way to becoming courageous, fearless, and decisive. Whenever we feel indecision and lack of courage, we must remind ourselves that life will end for us. The symbolic threat of death, which often is the cause of indecision, will then disappear, since its basic fraudulence will have been made manifest. We will be able once more to steer our life with courage and clarity.*

3. *By remembering the certainty and the finality of death, we immediately see the urgency of concentrating on essentials. We cut red tape in our life. We abandon excuses and procrastinations. We do not indulge in the luxury of wasting time—under the guise of getting work done—by getting lost in an endless amount of detail and busywork. Having not enough time is just a modernist affliction.*

4. *The vitality of death lies in that it makes almost impossible the repression of unpleasant but important realities. We do not accept any excuses to postpone dealing with our basic problems nor to hide these from ourselves. The realization of death carries with it the successful management of many unconscious and repressed problems. One who is about to die does not practice the art of self-deception. Death makes us honest.*

5. *To accept death means to take charge of one's life. One who sees the genuine function of death in life is no fatalist. They do not feel stuck or constrained. On the contrary, they are the freest of all. Fear is no longer an obstacle. There is nothing to be timid about, no reason to feel dependent, inadequate, or inferior; for we have once and for all conquered the ultimate threat. We have weaknesses and doubts, but that is part of being human.*

6. *The thought of death enables us to laugh off vicissitudes and pains. Every person has a certain type and amount of raw material out of which they can fashion for themselves a life. The amount and quality of that material varies greatly from one human existence to another and from one situation to another. But the pliable nature of the raw material is universal. To take defeat too seriously, to be thrown off balance by disappointments, is still secretly to harbor the hope that death may not be real after all and that perhaps the human race was meant to be immortal but, somehow, has missed its chance.*

Adapted from Peter Koestenbaum, *The Vitality of Death: Essays in Existential Psychology and Philosophy*, Westport, CT: Greenwood Publishing Co., 1971 (originally reprinted with permission from the *Journal of Existentialism*, no. 18 (Fall 1964): 139–166).

The presence of evil

Evil is not a word often used in organizations or even in community life. Perhaps the term is too religious or too black and white in a gray world. We are more comfortable talking about failure or obstacles or fate—even death—than evil. This is a symptom of a world that cares much more about whether something works well or poorly than whether something is right or wrong. Our avoidance of the word *evil* is another way language becomes political.

> "The concept of evil is generally avoided in conversations within organizations. Evil here is not a psychological perception as much as an undeniable reality. . . . Adjustment to evil is the denigration of the soul. Yet evil is real and remains real; the polarity of good and evil—witnessed with a clarity unequaled in the last century, at least in sheer numbers—is one of the most unbearable burdens of human existence."
>
> — Peter Koestenbaum (1978)

The reluctance to use the word *evil* in the commercial world or even in the civic or public service world is rather striking if you think about it. It precludes admission of guilt. It is not that we live without doubts and reservations about the things we do as an institution; it is just that there is no welcoming forum for expressing these doubts. There is no legitimacy in acknowledging our guilt. In fact, the opposite is true. It is rare that any organization acknowledges that it has done something wrong. They may, under pressure, pay restitution, but without admission of responsibility.

Our difficulty in acknowledging evil is akin to a lawyer's universal advice to a client in conflict: "Don't admit to anything and don't talk to anyone on the other side without me in the room." A modern version of hear no evil, see no evil, speak no evil.

Organizations are, in reality, containers of significant and painful human drama. Power is overdone by bosses and subordinates, people get aggressive and needlessly hurt others, our careers can get derailed, and we never get a chance to face our accuser. Companies act against the interests of their community or the larger society and can simply move on rather than be accountable. People get fired, even in good times, and sometimes for no reason other than they got a new supervisor. And on and on.

This is not an indictment against organizations, for they and we are human systems. We just want to introduce the discussion of structural harmful acts. It is a question of the willingness to acknowledge the harm. It is the denial of consequences that is significant. Systems and institutions avoid any accountability for harm and in that way we deny the existence of evil. *Evil* is a strong word, and not easy to use in institutional life. We are using the word here to make the point. Our unwillingness to use the word, especially in talking about ourselves and our workplaces, sanitizes conversation. That is why the decision to acknowledge the existence of evil by talking about it is a political act. It destabilizes the social structure in two ways: It goes against the code of denial in the organizational culture and also threatens to reimagine who has the power to define what is real and what is not real.

> *"Our freedom is capable of withstanding evil—of saying no to it. Our freedom is our only opportunity to choose to be noble, to stand up to evil, to counteract evil. The existential anxiety of evil reveals the preciousness of our freedom, and its enormous cosmic responsibility to uphold the values of civilization; it uncovers the much-neglected meaning of duty and obligation. These latter categories of ethics and morality are vital in bonding accountability with the experience of our freedom."*
> — *Peter Koestenbaum (1978)*

Denying the reality of evil

All this means that talking about the evil that is present in organizational life becomes risky business. In a high-control environment, the mindset often exists that either you are with us, or you are "not a team player." Or you are what is more popularly known in the extreme as a "whistle-blower." For a member of an institution to talk about institutional harm is to risk alienation.

In those rare cases where evil is acknowledged, our most common response is retribution. Find somebody to blame. If we can find one or two guilty parties and make an example of them, then the institution is exonerated. This search for

THEM, the need for a scapegoat, is another form of denial. The illusion is that those doing the investigative reporting, for example, are exonerated for being a factor in creating conditions for what they are exposing. They are innocent. It makes evil appear occasional and erasable.

> *"[E]vil is always there before us, demanding our attention. Evil deserves the respect, acknowledgment, and recognition given to a mad kidnapper or a grenade-packing terrorist on a crowded airplane. If we as much as blink our eyes, we have lost the sense of realism that our integrity requires, for in that fraction of a second we deluded ourselves that there are moments without evil. . . .*
>
> *"Our common response is to find fault. Blaming individuals, however, is a defense against being responsible for evil. If we find a culprit, we are momentarily relieved of apprehending the reality and absoluteness of evil. We think we have found the cause. And if we now eliminate it, we have eliminated evil from the world."*
>
> — *Peter Koestenbaum (1978)*

The cost of acting as if evil does not exist is that we are agreeing to live in and sustain a fictional environment—and through this we never really face the reality of the consequences of what we are engaged in. The denial of evil also takes a lot of time, money, and emotional energy to sustain. All of this makes it difficult to develop a culture of trust and authenticity when there are significant, unspeakable domains.

More important, when we lose sight of the presence of evil, we also lose its potential to keep us focused on purpose and to provoke its own restoration. Its restitution. In that way, we lose the redemptive power of evil. Plus, the denial of evil is what strengthens it.

"Any attempt to rationalize evil away is a tendency toward the denial of evil, whether we believe it leads to good or whether we feel that our struggle against it softens it. Only when we recognize evil as a final barrier do we experience the truth of our finitude. Only then do we live without illusion."

— *Peter Koestenbaum (1978)*

Do no harm

Another reason the discussion about evil is important is that harm does happen in organizational life. Harm is different from failure. Failure is a small death and means that something did not work. Harm means someone or some group acted to harm another. One of the insidious characteristics of evil is that it becomes so subtle that it defies much real notice and, over time, slowly works its way into the fabric of our expectations of organizational life. Cynicism is one of its more benign forms. So much so that we begin to think that it is normal and just the way the world works. It is what we call "reality." We deny it by implicitly agreeing that its effect is marginal and manageable and to be expected.

This kind of evil or harm is a form of the shadow that Carl Jung refers to. It is about abuse—the abuse of power, abuse of friendship, a promise knowingly broken and denied for the sake of self-interest, a story told that is true, but what is not told makes it a lie. It comes in the form of official announcements that no one believes. We spin messages to our own people; we present bad news in a way that sounds like we are still on plan and hopeful—as in the New Coke story.

Another example is that employees often first find out from the media, not from their own management, that their company or division is being shrunk, reorganized, or sold. Not a big deal, really—or is it?

These small indecencies on the surface are mildly harmful. But they build up and form a pattern of response that erodes community and accountability. In their nature they *are* evil, though in their form they are bland and disturbingly digestible. They are what makes institutional life so difficult and exasperating. The worst part about evil in organizations is that although harm is done daily, the institutions still work. They make money, serve customers and clients, perform well, and become larger. The fact that dark practices can be coincident with bright results is the paradox that grips us. This is especially vivid in the domain of marketing, where too often the incentive to purchase is in bright lights and the risks are in small type or very fast talking.

If, as insiders, we can acknowledge the existence of evil in organizational life, we won't eliminate it at all, but we will find ways to heal the wounds for those involved, which is all of us. We can collectively be aware of the harm being inflicted and need a way to deal with those actions as much as those who receive it. Fundamental to our purposes here is that evil is part of our humanity, which builds the character of individuals and institutions at the moment it is able to acknowledge its existence. For it is at this moment that the way is paved to confront it, which, successful or not, gives nobility not only to individuals, but also to our institutions and communities. And it creates the conditions where forgiveness is possible. And grief is understood. These are the action steps in the face of evil.

> *"[T]o be human is to struggle against evil. . . . Because of our polarized nature, we exist on the interface between good and evil. Our freedom chooses which side to take and how far to go. This type of choice is archetypal, basic, foundational. It defines who we are. The choice between good and evil is the choice between reason and unreason—and for that fundamental choice there is no good reason. Choosing between good and evil is choosing between the affirmations of life, consciousness, and freedom and their denials. To the extent that we opt for decency, we must look upon human existence as the permanent struggle against evil. A struggle we fight knowing we cannot win."*
>
> *— Peter Koestenbaum (1978)*

Implications: Failure, fear, death, and evil

I want to conclude this exploration of the value of dialoging with death and evil by summarizing how it can improve the quality of our organizational life. Death and evil are really questions, not conclusions. They force us to decide how to deal with the darker side of our experience and the world and markets within which we operate. When we make them legitimate questions, we are strengthened by their direct acknowledgment. What follows is an attempt to make this point as concrete as possible.

Small deaths

It is helpful to realize that every failure is experienced as a small death. We try to value failure as a learning experience, but it is a difficult stretch in most institutions. This may be due to the realization that if we accept failure, we accept the fact that something is going to die. If our intent is to find failure interesting and fascinating, and a source of learning and growth, then we have to come to terms with both our own death and the reality of our institution's mortality.

> *"The most dramatic reminder of our limitations, and of the decisive effect of them on finding meaning in life, is to be found in an understanding of the anticipation of death."*
> — Peter Koestenbaum (1971)

Institutional mortality means the organization will not go on forever. Neither will the unit we are a part of or the project we guide. Not only is it likely that the organization will have its own rhythm of ascension and decline—all an aspect of vitality—but elements and projects within it also live within a term limit. Any project we work on will reach a point where it is no longer supportable. It may be automated, disrupted, reduced for cost reasons. This has been exaggerated in the time of a pandemic. We need to accept that our work unit is a temporary structure and could at some point be merged into the very group that we wanted to take over. Plus, most of us will leave our current organization at some point, probably sooner rather than later. When we face the reality and presence of death, all of these smaller and symbolic versions of dying lose some of their paralyzing power. They have the potential to be taken as signs of life and a natural process rather than mistakes that should have been avoided.

> *"Only through the proper management of the threat of the death of myself—first in general and then in particular instances—will [you] be able to achieve genuine happiness and authentic success in [your] life."*
>
> — *Peter Koestenbaum (1971)*

To speak in these terms is usually frowned upon. We are all surrounded with false bravado: "Failure is not an option." The workplace becomes a place of manufactured optimism. We put posters on the wall with positive messages, we hold public meetings claiming a bright future and declaring success, and we then hold private meetings to deal with the reality of missed objectives or painful changes. This duality of public celebration and private realism is our defense against failure. This means we treat death as a mistake, as a sign that management has not done its job, or that workers have not acted accountably, or that technology has not reached its potential.

This denial of death in the form of failure has significant organizational costs. We keep investing in projects long after we know they will not succeed. We position news of a failure in a way that people will feel good about it, and thus create cultures of unreality and conscious or unconscious distrust. We also deny our guilt and avoid taking responsibility for failures, thus triggering widespread and long-term defensive reactions to events that could have been put to rest quickly if we could see them for what they were. . .simply failures.

The alternative is to take failures as gift-like reminders of the difficulty and impermanence of life and let this deepen our determination to invest in work that holds meaning and create organizations that we want to inhabit. We could then publicly acknowledge that something did not work. We would not need positioning language that shields people from the truth about their experience. For some unknowable reason, people did not particularly like the new Coke.

Time in a bottle

The moment we know we are going to die, we become aware of the subjective nature of time. Time is more of an experience than a chronological truth. How long is a "long time"? To a child an hour is an eternity; to an older person, a year races by. When we are in the dentist's chair, each minute drags on; when we are in love or on vacation, whole days disappear in a flash. In modern culture, speed has become a god, a value in its own right. We need to be on call and instantly responsive. We accept as a fact, not a choice, that it is better to do things faster. After all, time is money. Time waits for no one. Time marches on.

This passion for speed is a way of getting rid of time, not valuing time as precious, scarce, and something to be savored. There is a confusion between running out of time and therefore doing now what I might have postponed until later and doing everything at breakneck speed. Speed obliterates or blurs the quality of our experience and makes relationships obsolete. In the speed world, we do not have time for anything that moves at human rather than electronic speed. It is a convenience culture. Convenient news, entertainment, food, and consumption. In the conversational commerce world we try to eliminate "friction," which is code for eliminating all direct human contact in our transactions with our brands or customers. Even the belief that I will make my money or my number now, doing work that has little meaning, and then later enjoy the luxury of doing what I want, is a bet on living forever. Every act of postponement is a belief in immortality.

So, in a paradoxical way, our awareness of our own death makes time more valuable and speed a liability. It is intriguing that youth is in a hurry when they have so much time in front of them and maturity slows things down when time is running out. An institutional passion for speed may be partly a sign of its immaturity, caught in youth's experience of time, unable to see that anything done with depth and purpose takes time, even if we think we do not have it. To know how temporary and passing each thing we do is allows us to accept that any projects or experience that will have a significant impact will take time, even more than we think we have. At this point, "How long will it take?" will be the fourth question we ask, instead of the first.

Saying no and the value of dissent

Death is the ultimate finality. It is the final and nonnegotiable limitation. It is life's most emphatic way of saying no to us. No wonder that we have such difficulty in saying no. It is the reminder that we cannot do everything, that many of our

dreams will not be fulfilled, that we are in fact going to die.
The effect is that no matter how full our plate, we act as if
there is room for one more helping.

This is pronounced in institutional life. We have this belief
that if you stand up you will get shot. We make the association
between standing up—which really means to say no by
publicly disagreeing with those in power—and extreme
danger. We believe that the messenger will be shot, and
therefore a refusal is equivalent to an act of suicide. This is not
just in business, it is common in churches, hospitals,
monasteries, and ashrams.

Our resolution of this dilemma is to not say no. To present
ourselves as a "can do" kind of person. More team player
mythology. In one bank, it came down to the question, "Are
you with us, or are you a terrorist?" When this is the choice,
saying no is an understandably rare occurrence.

Our unwillingness to say no is a denial of our limitations,
a refusal to acknowledge our mortality and the fact that there
are some things we cannot do. It also expresses our willingness
to allow others to define reality for us. Declaring no is also the
first act of reclaiming our freedom. It is deciding for ourselves
what is real and possible and worth pursuing. To think that
saying no is a disaster is the choice to remain a child with all
the beliefs that those who have power over us are all-knowing.
They aren't; they just have power over us.

Making refusal so difficult has its institutional costs. It
makes our promises and goals inherently unstable. We create

expectations we know at the time we cannot fulfill, and so the organizational promises, based on our promises, are unstable and at risk from their inception. It may be true that setting goals beyond reason may have a motivating effect and cause us to stretch and grow in ways we otherwise might not. This would be valuable, however, only if people chose to set high goals, not if they acceded to them out of fear of saying no.

If we want to actually live in the real world, we have to accept no for an answer. As managers, we might even encourage refusal and value people saying no. We can start to do this if we realize that saying no is the beginning of a conversation, not the end of a conversation. It is an equalizing stance, a way to begin as partners. Partners say no to us, and we survive. Every work unit has its limitations, is going to fail at times, is not going to live forever, and therefore has to ground its promises in reality. When we can accept the importance of saying no, we accept the presence of death, and then become grounded in our commitments. There may be negative consequences to this stance, but we will survive, and the payoff is that we know at that moment that we stand for something, that we are experiencing our freedom.

Finally, when we accept that it is not certain that the institution will survive, we will live more fully and create organizations that are more human and habitable. This means we leave room for the possibility of ending and returning in another form. Death is a precursor to rebirth. If we sincerely care about our institutions and what they stand for, we can live with this mindset.

"Surprisingly, death as a mental presence can be relaxing, fascinating, and entertaining, in addition to showing its more common characteristics of horror, dread, despair, and tragedy."
— Peter Koestenbaum (1971)

The wish to improve and transform our institutions without any loss, without any ending or any serious transformation, devalues them. It condemns them to remain economic shells whose only purpose is financial, operational, and success through scale. Real transformation is of the spirit, not the form. Something gets completed and returns in a more vibrant form, and this occurs within organizational journeys, neighborhood narratives, as well as individual ones.

Social responsibility

The existence of evil asks us to take purpose and meaning seriously. It gives rise to morality and an ethical stance. The philosophic insight takes a broad look at what is defined as evil. It includes more than the more traditional ethical business practices of accurate reporting, playing it straight on pricing, diversity, workplace safety, and product safety. And personal practices of harm, alienation, and manipulation.

The dominant values in most businesses and public sector organizations are growth, margins, and efficiency. They value what works, often at the expense of what has meaning and what a wider view of social responsibility might entail. What the existence of evil raises for institutions is the question of their purpose and larger responsibility to the world around them. For the private sector, the economic eye, with Milton Friedman and the Chicago School of Economics as the placeholder, holds the view that any stance that does not contribute to the bottom line is acting against the interests of the stockholders. At least until the post-Friedman era. For government, the question of what sector of society it exists to serve is very complicated and ambiguous. Churches and not for profits likewise face the question of who they exist to serve. They have endowments whose trustees believe that their primary obligation is to sustain the endowment. To use only 5 percent of it to distribute. An option would be to expand its use in hard economic times rather than contract its giving because of lower earning returns on the wealth. Plus, should they think of themselves as being in competition with other organizations like themselves?

Another example is that in the private sector, what does it mean that the philanthropic giving of organizations used to be controlled by community affairs departments and now it is increasingly controlled by the marketing department? Should donations be based on where the most public visibility can be achieved? And are the benefactors of their generosity limited to the market segment that they serve? Books like *Toxic Charity* (Lupton 2011) and *Decolonizing Wealth* (Villanueva 2021) raise the question of the use and purpose of wealth.

At some point organizations will view economic disparity, community, and social well-being as a central concern of the institution. The private sector is increasingly powerful in the political arena and in many cases, organizations transcend cities, states, and even nations as political entities. What does this mean for their role in addressing problems that used to be the sole province of government and public agencies? The existence of evil on a wider scale is fast becoming an organizational and business issue.

The leading edge of social responsibility

Here are some forms of accountability and possibility that are on the horizon for places that will come to value freedom and accountability over constraint and predictability and institutions that will increasingly treat social impact as equivalent to outcomes and surplus:

- Urban prosperity. The decay of our central urban areas is a growing crisis. Many companies have committed themselves to supporting urban revitalization, but when they do, it too often becomes displacement, which is replacing old architecture, occupied by lower-income citizens, with modern multistory buildings. And this is called development. Companies have often led the flight from central areas of a city, or an at-risk region, to move to less developed, lower-cost areas that offer short-term economic benefits. As long as a company believes it exists primarily to make a profit, this will never change.
- Companies have worked hard to reduce labor costs and benefit packages for the core workers, while maintaining good incentives and packages for the top management. This continues to include active anti-union efforts, strong stances against wage increases, and outsourcing or exporting as many jobs as possible. We have witnessed the

end of defined benefit pension plans. Are these issues of morality or just good business practices?

- Some businesses are the most outspoken critics of government regulations and interference yet have little compunction against using their job-creating power to negotiate all kinds of tax and regulatory concessions when deciding where to expand or relocate. There is language in every city of public–private partnerships. What this means is public funding for private enterprise. At what point will the private sector and government believe in a balance of power and recognize that they need each other? This does occur, but they are still the exception.

- What about the environment? There is a great deal written about how businesses externalize their costs by asking the community to carry the cost of things such as production and packaging waste, environmental harm, uses destructive to the land, and the creation and maintenance of a supportive infrastructure (roads, police, fire, schools, and the like). Something will shift when our organizations act on their interdependence and accept that in the longer term all costs will be borne by all of us. Thankfully this shows some signs of shifting.

- As part of the globalization surge, what commitment do organizations have toward the community and cultural integrity of countries they do business in? What does it mean to sell consumerism and all of its values and qualities to developing, southern hemisphere and African countries? To India and more? As an example, for whose sake do we try to convince Indonesians to substitute soft drinks for tea, juice, and water?

- Despite the existence of truth-in-advertising rules, what about the promises made in our efforts to sell products? Will a car give the freedom that the selling effort promises?

Will products really help us age happily, enjoy financial security in our golden years, create happy children, and fill our lives with glamour and excitement? Marketing could be a vehicle for integrating the well-being of the institution with the well-being of us all. There are beginnings of this in the interracial faces of the people we see. In the social service world, this would take the form of creating a new narrative of the gifts of those we care most about. Ending stories of need and deficiencies and beginning stories of the accomplishments and capacities of those who are neighbors of infinite capacity and infinite abilities to sustain their cultures. Plus we need to stop labelling people by their annual income or where they are sleeping tonight. This is not who they are. There is no such thing as a homeless person. Calling them people who experience homelessness is still too small a version of a person.

- What about the impact of superstores and low-cost online convenience? Might we all place value on the viability of local communities and local economies? Is the economic independence of a community something an organization or local government need worry about? And what about business and housing development practices? What does it mean when we consider raw land useless because we cannot build on it? This is the basis of most urban planning. When did we stop caring about the end of the family farm and the impact on rural communities? Thank you, Wendell Berry.

- And when will we willingly come to terms with our distrust and exploitation of the other? Economic equity is a simple term for it. We have and currently receive advantages from our desire for low labor costs. Slavery in its old and current forms. Our penchant to treat African

Americans and people of color and immigrants as
strangers. Stop the patronizing ways of mild recognition
with Black leadership positions and diversity vice
presidents. It is an economic issue that has nothing to do
with highly placed individuals.

It is not that organizations are the evil we must work to
overcome or that organizations are to blame for the existence
of these problems. These questions are simply a short list of
some of the challenges that the reality of the world presents
to us. We are each participating in creating these issues. Plus, it
is each of us who populates the organizations that too often
become easy to blame. Evil is the other face, the hard face of
reality that insolubly presents itself to us and will not go away.
Such is the nature of these dilemmas. They are ones, however,
that institutions are capable of speaking to and making the
conversation at the center of their intentions.

If anything is to shift in how we think and deal with evil,
there has to be a shift in intent. Is there a vital place in our
institutional life for us to do things just because they are right,
and simply that? We have experience in doing the right thing;
we just need to expand it. A small example was in the quality
movement, where for a while we did what was right for the
customer, gave the employee more choice, and cost and habit
were secondary concerns.

Philosophy urges us to value the ideas of evil and mortality.
To own and embrace them, despite the discomfort of the
words. We have the capacity to acknowledge our place in the
dark and shadow side of ourselves as an individual, and we can

speak this in our institutional world, and this ennobles the meaning of work and our institutions. This is different from simply defending ourselves against evil or death, deluding ourselves in thinking we can eradicate them. Even making the term "evil" acceptable language in the workplace would be a step in this direction.

> *"It makes us realize—if but for a fraction of an unpleasant moment—that the world in which we live, with its goals, prejudices, and institutions, is not the solid existence that we had believed and hoped."*
>
> — *Peter Koestenbaum (1971)*

4

Fully Human
Organizations

We now begin to bring together the elements of what we are calling the philosophic insight. In writing on this topic, we want to take on some very practical, though profound, implications of our freedom. The philosopher elaborates on the inescapable guilt of self-betrayal and how this existential guilt actually makes personal and organizational freedom possible. We are caught in the caldron of sorting through roles the culture defines for us—in other words, what life expects of us—and then turning this question back on itself to ask what we expect of life. In the end, when we decide to absorb the full meaning of what it is to be free, we have to come to terms with the internal and external struggle that constantly faces us. We can do this individually and, more important, collectively in the institutions and communities where we gather.

> "The primacy of our here-and-now consciousness and the freedom to choose one's own role are philosophic fundamentals about human existence which, if understood, can reintroduce harmony into the lives of many people."
>
> — Peter Koestenbaum (1978)

Guilty as chosen and guilty as charged

One of the major shifts in my own thinking about accountability has to with guilt. This was the recognition that much of the guilt I have lived with has been well founded—that to be human is to live with the experience of a particular kind of guilt, that which arises from acts of self-betrayal and becoming the person that others wish us to be. That the origin story of accountability has to do with being accountable to ourselves, as individuals and as members of a community or institution. This begins the story we hold about ourselves.

The philosophic insight distinguishes between two kinds of guilt: the existential guilt of betraying our own capacity to be fully ourselves and fully human, and the neurotic guilt of adapting ourselves to what we believe the world expects of us. If you can accept this idea for a moment and look at our modern organizations, you get a sense of how powerful our organizations are in reinforcing our neurotic guilt. And you see how difficult they (and we) make it to act on our existential guilt and choose to bring our full selves into our place of work.

> *"An important revelation of existential anxiety is the understanding of two kinds of guilt. . . . In brief, existential guilt is guilt about unfulfilled potential, about self-betrayal, and anger at one's weakness. Neurotic guilt has two layers: the denial of the existence of existential guilt altogether, and the internalization of external and essentially irrelevant rules and values."*
> — *Peter Koestenbaum (1978)*

Here are simply a few of the more obvious ways even the best and healthiest organizations reinforce our neurotic instinct to fit in and adapt ourselves into what the institution and, through it, the larger culture, expects of us. Here are some forms of institutionalization:

1. **Performance and reward systems.** We conduct performance appraisals in which the ways we should change in order to "be successful" are made painfully explicit. Managers are required to appraise each subordinate and

identify areas of individual improvement. Strengths and weaknesses are noted and documented. Money is then tied to this feedback in order to put full weight on what our management wants us to become. Asking a person, "What do you want to become and how can we adapt to help you be that?" is rare. Even if these questions are asked in some form, it is secondary to the discussion of what the institution expects of us and how it feels about who we are. Three-sixty-degree feedback is one delivery system for this. Feedback can be valuable, but when sought, not required.

2. **Institutionalized values.** Institutions define the values we are to live by. Management publishes "aspirations" and "core values," as if without them, we would live by values that would undermine or defeat the organization. It is hard to conceive why an adult human being would seek from others a set of values to live by. When corporate values are defined by the few for the many, it reinforces the neurotic guilt that lies within us.

"Every institution operates with a set of norms and expects its members to live by them. In other words, they have a fixed notion of what normal behavior is and in fact value it, even treat it as a given. The philosophic insight suggests that the word 'normal' has absolutely no meaning when applied to either a person's life or their relationship to leadership and power. The meaninglessness of normalcy is not a value or disvalue but a philosophically disclosed, existential fact. Normalcy is a chosen value or the commitment to a value; it is not a fact."

— Peter Koestenbaum (1971)

3. **Prescribed training.** We conduct training programs that are highly prescriptive of desired behavior. As designers of training events, we begin by asking what kind of behaviors

we want these participants to leave the training with. In our well-intentioned effort to provide meaningful learning experiences, we deliver the message that our employees are not enough as they are, and we have the answer to that. Now, many training programs support the full development of the person in their content, but when they are prescribed, name competencies, and individuals are "nominated" to attend, those acts carry the message that our future is in someone else's hands. And then it is our neurotic guilt that leads us to be grateful for the nomination and attentive to what they have in mind for us.

"The person who is guided and directed towards an externally anchored self-concept has relinquished and lost their freedom; in truth, they have lost . . . [themselves. Abdicated their] inner humanity, integrity, ego, and 'self.' . . . [Capitulated] to an external object which we must become, rather than to exercise the freedom which we are."

— *Peter Koestenbaum (1971)*

4. **Reinforcing our wish for safety and a predictable future.** What is most disturbing about practices that reinforce neurotic guilt is that we, as employees, ask for them. We all want to know what our supervisor or manager thinks of us. We ask for ways we should improve. We are looking for a prescription to provide some surety about our future. We want institutional mentors, a plan for our development.

We need help from others, but from those we choose, and for a future we will construct. One focused on meaning rather than job title. One of the promises of the philosophic insight is that human beings are inherently capable of creating lives of meaning and service. We see that each of us has the capacity to use our freedom in service of an institution and that this service does not have to be trained, prescribed, and coached into us. When we get this, in fact, organizations will be able to be even more demanding of its members. It will expect people to be accountable, to find their own meaning, and to look failure in the eye. Managers will find great relief in ending their penance of caretaking and nurturing their subordinates into personhood.

"[I]f a person fails at work, it is the decision to fail that is at the root of the matter. Once a real decision to succeed has been made— and the full, multilevel structure of that free personal decision must be understood in a philosophical and not in a commonsense manner—then the work and organization will automatically succeed. Part of the reason for its success will be a redefinition of success itself."

— *Peter Koestenbaum (1971)*

It is the existence of existential guilt that makes the dream of creating cultures of freedom and accountability possible. I am guilty because I choose to live, choose to say no to certain people and choices. To say yes to pursuing deeper purpose in whatever requirements are required for the whole system to succeed, I, along with peers, decide how to make this moment, this meeting, the way of occupying this room examples of the world we want to inhabit. This is what freedom looks like.

The sounds of freedom

One other implication of this way of viewing guilt: It adds one more evocative word to use in our effort to change our language in order to change our culture. When we add the language of guilt to the language of freedom, death, anxiety, and evil, it personalizes and deepens our cultural ways of being together. It recognizes that institutions are profoundly human systems, not mechanical or super-rational systems.

This language, because of its evocative power, allows us to construct an alternative narrative. Alters the way we define what is worth talking about. By redefining what we talk about and how we talk about it, we change our experience and come one step closer to making our institutions less rigid and more effective in adapting quickly and more realistically to their environment. Using this language—and thereby the power of its philosophical content—will also work to make our workplaces more democratic and habitable. And it confronts and strengthens us in becoming more congruent in how we decide to inhabit them.

What this requires is a change in the order of the questions we gather around. We begin with questions of individual and collective purpose. We create space for dissent and doubt. We talk about what role we have individually and collectively played in creating the challenge of the moment. We ask each other what promises we are willing to make. We discuss the gifts we bring to this situation and this team. And then, maybe, we discuss what actions we plan to take. Maybe even make a list.

Reversing the illusion of clear roles and expectations

When we engage the question of what the world expects of us, we typically think that if we can be clear about roles, it will facilitate their fulfillment. This instinct is particularly evident when institutions try to change themselves or try to resolve some of their inherent internal conflicts. We consistently turn to role definition as the universal solvent. We are constantly trying to define people's roles: What is the new role of middle management, and what is the role of a manager in an empowered environment? In creating new products and services, what is the role of the marketing group and what is the role of the research group? This is of course reasonable and needed, but we give it more power than it serves us. Our belief seems to be that we can find resolution for much of the complexity of organizational and communal life by the mere definition of roles.

"We are fundamentally free to define the precise role of work in our search for meaning—but we are also fully responsible for the consequences of our definition."
— *Peter Koestenbaum (1971)*

From a philosopher's viewpoint, however, role clarity as a solution is best achieved when the players themselves contract over boundaries and responsibilities. Of course, some role definition is essential and foundational. It is when it is not working that the institution thinks it can legislate a resolution. The option is to have conversations of promises to peers. Commitments to outcomes. This promotes localized exchanges rather than centralized definitions.

A dramatic example of the belief that it is a good thing to prescribe a job function, or role, or pedagogy can be found in public schools' attempts at standardized curricula. This is taken to the point where a state legislature or department requires that our children are taught a dictated curriculum, enforced by standardized testing.

> *"[A] role is an image some people have of themselves. Its structure is clear and it cannot be easily changed or eradicated. Such role-images are an independent force in our lives. We did not create the image; it appeared on its own, and its binding power is irrefutable. The reality is, however, that it is not possible to fulfill completely and satisfactorily the demands of one role, much less of all of them. The consequence of this inevitable frustration is a sense of futility, worthlessness, and guilt that seems to become an ineradicable part of life. We inevitably recognize the discrepancy between the real and the ideal, and the resulting pain, if faced, can be unendurable."*
> — *Peter Koestenbaum (1971)*

Not enough

The struggle, though, is how each of us confronts the reality that we are not going to live out the role expectations that society has in mind for us. The competency model is just one of the most explicit, and extreme, forms of how the culture demands that we fit into the frame of their expectations. In school we call it "socialization." These expectations are held in good will, and usually, as in the case of the competency model, they are based on reasoned observation and orderly thinking about what actions best serve the institution. But the challenge is that they may be interesting but are not powerful.

The fact is that, try as we might, we are inevitably going to disappoint these expectations. How we deal with this crisis is the focus of some of Peter's writing on freedom and suffering. From a philosophical viewpoint, the fact we will disappoint—or to use a stronger word, betray—those around us is, in fact, not a failure, but the beginning of finding our own path, our own voice, our own definition of ourselves.

> *"[W]e always exist in a particular set of circumstances; these conditions limit us severely and we have limited control over them. The extent of our control over our life situation is at best to shift from one set of situations to another. But from the perspective of our quest for ultimate satisfaction, that is no solace."*
> — *Peter Koestenbaum (1971)*

As mentioned previously, being explicit about roles has value when it becomes the beginning of a conversation rather than becoming a standard for measurement. When we can accept the fact that we will never comfortably fit within the roles that are defined for us, we create space in our institutions for the mystery and beauty of human variation. The institutional fear is that if people do not function within defined roles, chaos will result and the goals of the organization will not be met. The opposite may be true. One definition of bureaucracy is that it is a world in which people are rule or role bound. In schools, teachers must teach to the standardized test. No exceptions are allowed without time-consuming approvals, where local variation and local choice are defined out of existence.

To create entrepreneurial or adaptive institutions, violating roles and crossing boundaries are essential. And this is the reality of how things actually get done. One of the reasons we feel most useful and alive in a crisis is that for a short period of time, the rules are suspended. Ask anyone with the job of restoring electricity in a storm. Hierarchy is suspended to both be safe and serve the community. We move our organizations forward when we accept this as daily life and treat roles as instructional possibilities that are constantly changing. The temporary quality of roles and the tension between how we have designed a way of operating and how we keep changing it are signs of vitality. This a major attraction of working at home.

Conflict with the expectations presented to us also becomes a source of character and meaning for us as individuals. Carl Jung has stated that all consciousness begins with an act of disobedience. He also declared that all compassion begins with a broken heart. Philosophy brings us the fruits of this theme.

Our expectations

We not only have to live with meeting or disappointing the expectations of those around us, but we have to face our own disappointments. It is one thing to know that you were not exactly the child that your parents had in mind, but it is also true that for a significant segment of your life, your parents did not quite fit the image of what you thought you needed or deserved.

Philosophy offers the insight that these failures or disappointments are not problems to be solved or signs of weaknesses in ourselves or others or reciprocal demands to be negotiated. These disappointments are in the nature—the human nature—of things. Most workplaces are breeding grounds for unfulfilled expectations, which easily turn into resentment. Too often we expect things from the institution and its leaders that were unfulfilled for us as children. We want our bosses to be congruent, to walk their talk, to get along well together. We want to be the favorite employee, just as we wished to be the favorite child. There is no more constant and plaintive cry heard from employees than the wish for their bosses to be something more, something different. They claim their bosses don't communicate about what the future looks like. Where we are headed. Where is the space for bosses to simply say, "We don't know"?

> *"Managers create a relationship with great learning potential, if they can share with the employee their own anxieties about their relationship, their own inadequacies in their role and way of relating to subordinates."*
>
> — *Peter Koestenbaum (1978)*

The gap between what our workplace is and what we wish it to be gives meaning to our being there. Even if we are there only two days a week. It creates a vacuum that can only be filled through the discovery of our freedom and accepting the accountability to re-found our institutions to become places we wish to inhabit. Our institutions are transformed the moment we decide they are ours to create.

This is a difficult insight to absorb. It is hard to abandon the belief that the organization and its leaders could provide us more of what we desire, if they would just choose to do so. If we really trust the message of our experience, we are forced to take back into our own selves what we had been expecting from our leaders. The reality is that our leaders are right now giving us all they are capable of giving. They are not withholding anything. They see the longing in our eyes, do what they can to fulfill those longings, and still fall short. And each of us, as leaders or in any other aspect of our lives, home or away, do the same.

> *"Managers who take on these expectations or internalize unwarranted demands either have no inner-directed sense for their own self-image—and thus depend entirely for what they think they are on how others perceive them—or they have the need to think of themselves as a kind of god."*
>
> — *Peter Koestenbaum (1978)*

The problem is that the moment we finally accept the limitations of our leaders as permanent and unchanging, as inevitable, we lose our sense of security. This loss can be overwhelming, partly because it reminds us of the safety that childhood promised us and did not deliver. The wish for safety is so strong that many of us will still choose to believe that a change in those around us is possible and required for us to be satisfied. This is the nature of the struggle. This is also true in the political realm, but that is another conversation.

These questions are discussed in their most elemental form under the rubric of the "problem of meaning." It is in talking about our humanity in terms of suffering, death, fate, and boundaries that we come closer to seeing clearly what is at stake for us. Again, the power of the uncompromising language of the philosopher is what we need to allow the reality of our experience to penetrate through our defenses against an existence that we did not call for and the feeling that it is more than we can handle.

> *"Existentialism holds the view that we are by nature alienated and anxious, that our existence is constantly threatened by a sense of meaninglessness, and that despair is often just around the corner. [We claim our freedom when] we begin to see the intimate connection that exists between the anxiety and guilt of meaninglessness and the discovery of genuine meaning in life."*
> — *Peter Koestenbaum (1971)*

What are we to do?

To tie all the threads together we return to where we began, an understanding of what it means to be free. To have free will. The moment we accept our complete and absolute freedom, it is easy to understand why we resist this profound and disturbing insight. My freedom declares me to be accountable for my experience and stance for every aspect of my life.

> *"We must recognize that the size of the work is part of the definition of work regarding which we are both free and responsible—and accountable, for the consequences are now part of the real world."*
> — *Peter Koestenbaum (1971)*

This means that all my complaints, my judgments, and my rationalizations for my condition become hollow and without any basis in fact. They are indeed satisfying, but not useful. I have created my version of my own story, from day one years ago and into the future.

To make this more explicit, it means that, at work, I accept that I have constructed and imagined what kind of management runs my organization. I choose what I need from the institution and place in my own hands how I will be satisfied or disappointed. I have been the determining force behind what I have been rewarded and punished for.

There is an objective reality out there—my institution does have a certain culture, others do act to create that culture, management and colleagues do in fact act in a way that impacts me—but none of it gives me an excuse or explanation for the quality and texture of my own experience or my own choices. They choose their actions; I choose my response.

There is, of course, a cost to claiming my freedom and wearing my accountability. I have to give up the desire to live within the protection of longing for a normal life. I have to live with this form of anxiety. As Peter explains it, there is no such thing as normalcy. The old normal wasn't normal. There are only the cards that lie on the table before me.

"The philosophic insight suggests that the word 'normal' has absolutely no meaning when applied to either a person's life or their relationship to leadership and power. The meaninglessness of normalcy is not a value or disvalue but a philosophically disclosed,

existential fact. Normalcy is a chosen value or the commitment to a value; it is not a fact . . . the prevalent uses of 'normalcy' and 'need' are, strictly speaking, meaningless."
— Peter Koestenbaum (1971)

This version of a pathway to freedom also causes us to question what psychology has taught us, namely that that we have certain basic needs, and these needs drive our behavior. What psychology has defined as needs now become choices. If we can accept this, then it changes our thinking about everything. We stop treating management as the cause of employee behavior. Managers are no longer responsible for the morale or even the performance of their subordinates. Also, managers can stop explaining their own behavior as a response to "feedback" and expectations. Managers stop thinking they are growing and developing "their" people. This opens space to be partners, colleagues, members of a team with special responsibilities. Setting context, requirements for outcomes, conveners of conversations among the team about where we stand, how we are working together, and what we want from each other. Real work but stripped of colonial and parenting garments. It leaves boss and subordinates with the awesome task of either confronting people with their freedom or supporting their escape from it.

"If the employee opts for the real-and-authentic view, the manager's individuality and freedom become the true and freely accepted limits to the employee's individuality and freedom."
— Peter Koestenbaum (1971)

Interestingly, this shift in thinking may not so much change our behavior with subordinates or with bosses; instead, it changes the context in which we operate. We continue to support, reward, and influence people, but we do it out of our own sense of what is right and wrong. We do those things as an ethical stance, or a philosophical stance, rather than as a motivational strategy. We construct processes that are transparent and as fair as possible. High performers should definitely make more money, but we do not have to rank order people or stamp a number or letter grade on their forehead.

As employees, the moment we accept our freedom, we stop treating leaders and managers as if they were so important. We hope they are smart about the business we are in, but they are no longer the cause of our satisfaction or our performance. They just exist as partners or colleagues to be dealt with, as does all that comes toward us in life. My anxiety, my willingness to accept the fact that I am running out of time, my guilt for what possibilities I have not yet fulfilled, all belong to me and the subjective manner in which I have constructed or constituted my own experience. This is at the center of an alternative story I can live into.

This act of accountability becomes the source of my own power. It also leaves me with the experience of being alone, much more deeply and profoundly than I have been prepared to accept. All the more reason for the conversations that build belonging. The weight of this accountability may be one reason why the typical workplace conversation talks more of boundaries than of freedom, and why parenting is so much more attractive than partnering, and why we have embraced the economist's belief that behavior can be bartered and our relationships with one another comprise a marketplace in which we constantly exchange and balance needs and offers. Quid pro quo life.

"In sum, understanding freedom means nothing without understanding responsibility and accountability."
— *Peter Koestenbaum (1971)*

Regardless of the extent to which we accept the centrality of our freedom, the question of our freedom is at the center of how we conceptualize and design our collective endeavors. The organizational structures and practices we have inherited reflect a low opinion of our capacity to claim our freedom and use it accountably. We have acted on the belief that people need leadership, need direction, need to be nurtured, trained, and coached into high performance. Bureaucracy is, in effect, an escape from freedom. It is an institutionalized longing for a world of safety and predictability. If we wanted to eliminate bureaucracy, as we say we do, it can be done in an instant. We need only to stop believing it is necessary. Plus, we are surrounded with examples of people seeking the alternative. Self-managing teams. Open-space ways of being together. Quality circles. Flat structures. Offices that erase status as an interior design principle. Peer accountability structures. Choices in where we work and when to gather. All of these are available to us and more. Waiting to be chosen as central to our way of being together rather than interesting experiments that ebb and flow with the times.

" . . . we escape [freedom] through pursuits such as busy-work and games that temporarily keep our minds off the real issues of human existence."

— *Peter Koestenbaum (1971)*

If we insist on the importance of strong leadership, then we can have that in an instant also. All we have to do is provide it. Or choose to believe that those currently in power will change their use of that power the moment we are ready for them to do so.

Real and chosen accountability? Fully human organizations

We began with the idea that our freedom carries its own requirements. The reward for structuring to support freedom is the accountability it produces. This accountability has its own physiology. This includes existential guilt, which is guilt about unfulfilled potential, about self-betrayal, and anger at one's weakness. Its cousin is neurotic guilt, which has two layers: "the denial of the existence of existential guilt altogether, and the internalization of external and essentially irrelevant rules and values."

This insight is like a laser beam into one of the most pressing questions of organizational life: "Can I be myself and still be successful?" For most of us, the answer is "maybe" at best, and if you look at our actions, the answer is "no." We believe that work is someplace where we cannot be ourselves. We reserve nights and weekends to be ourselves and believe that our place of employment is reserved for a narrower version of who we are—that's why we call it "work." Again the appeal of working at home. A place where I have a better chance of being myself.

Last time about guilt

What is interesting about the philosophic insight is that it proposes that we are going to feel guilty, no matter what. It is a feature, if not a benefit, of being alive and human. So the questions become: What kind of guilt do we choose for ourselves? And what do we believe best supports others?

If we believe that an accountable culture comes from the experience of freedom, we would look for ways to support people to be more of themselves. We would adopt strategies of invitation and consent. It would entail stronger listening, deeper and more personal dialogue, self-defined learning goals, and a focus on strengths rather than deficiencies.

The specifics could take a hundred forms, but the simple question of how an institution confronts people with their freedom and asks them to bring all of themselves to work would form the basis of a new conversation. This would begin a shift toward a liberating experience of membership. This brings questions of deeper purpose and community well-being to the center of institutional life. These are most often relegated to special occasions and lean on consultants to tell us what our peer groups are doing.

The opportunity of meaning

The philosophic insight challenges us to be more fully human and requires us to more courageously confront the meaning of our existence. Organizations are a major playing field on which meaning is likely to be found. The challenge is to engage in this pursuit collectively rather than individually. Institutions are something more than collections of individual purposes. They force the question of what we want to create together, taking the focus off what I want to create individually. This is in contrast to the domains of psychology, religion, and social services, which are primarily focused in the individual and their development and transcendence.

In this individualistic culture, we have a difficult time thinking about the collective. We are actually afraid of it. We have created the negative imagery of communism and socialism to symbolize our fear of losing our individuality, of putting our love of the spirit of capitalism and individual freedom at risk. We fear groupthink and group pressure. Naming these fears serves to reinforce the passion for consistency, control, and predictability. The superpower of capitalism and colonialism.

At the same time, we have evidence and appreciation for the idea of community. There is in each of us a longing to belong to something larger than ourselves, to come together in common purpose. A group or organization with a compelling vision begins to answer our questions about purpose, meaning, destiny. In this way, we can think of institutions as well as individuals as being created in God's image, or perhaps that of a higher power. We can accept the existence of community destiny in modern times, or the spiritual pursuit of a lost tribe or a "people" in ancient times. This is the importance of indigenous cultures. This kind of thinking—and the difficulty and resistance we experience when we engage in it—brings life to our institutions.

The need for a larger and compelling purpose is especially important in a materialistic and entitlement culture where the dominant question is, "What's in it for me?" This question signals the death of community and meaning. Every organization has the possibility of defining a meaning for itself that enlivens and animates a collective longing. To say that this organization is in business to make money, or to deliver a specific service, is becoming too narrow to be sustaining.

What is key is the dialogue about purpose rather than the expectation that there is a final answer. The engineer in us wants a specific answer that will last, but this treats meaning as if it were a goal, an object. Which treats ourselves as objects and our relationships as instrumental. Meaning is found in the struggle with the question, in the dialogue with others, in facing the futility of trying to express in a phrase something that is larger than any of us and essentially unnameable.

It is interesting that many corporations, in engaging the question of deeper purpose, return to the insights of the founder many years ago. Forrest Mars talked about the importance of mutuality. Heineken returns to the language of the joy of being together. This speaks of deeper purpose, where money is simply a means, as are key performance indicators. A larger, overarching purpose always resides in our own history, if we choose to look closely. And even when we hold the language of that purpose, we can begin to put aside all the habits and practices that distract from the essential and existential point.

> *"We do have a nature, but it is not made up of irreducible needs. It consists of intentional consciousness, the meaning-giving power of our own acts of awareness, which is a vast and threatening region of existential freedom."*
>
> — *Peter Koestenbaum (1971)*

It also comes in facing and acknowledging the suffering and complexity of belonging to a community or an organization. In one sense, organizational meaning is experienced in exploring all the questions that this book raises for us. It recognizes that freedom and accountability are questions that we will never answer satisfactorily.

If we can tolerate questions of this nature, the character of our organizations will start to shift. Institutions will become places where we expect to struggle with life's deeper questions, and we will discover that we can delve deeply and not only survive, but also get work done. It will give an importance to our workplaces and in fact raise our expectations of what they can become. It is at this point that we will begin to believe that we can be ourselves and also be successful.

"In our work lives the fear of suicide comes in coded form, which is the fear of being fired—and especially the fear of being fired because we dared to truly be ourselves."

— *Peter Koestenbaum (1971)*

The entrepreneurial act of creation

Existential philosophy assumes we are capable of the act of creation—that we have, whether we admit it or not, created the world in which we live, the workplace included. The possibility of creating our own world actually finds a friend in our organizational experience. The entrepreneurial archetype or instinct is a major contribution that organizations, especially businesses, make to the culture.

Capitalism's great strength is the opportunity to create an organization from nothing. It is a stunning form of societal freedom that we are right to defend. Every organization we belong to started with simply an idea. Words on paper or a wall. It began as an idea in someone's mind or garage, and they not only had the thought, but also the will and sense of their own freedom to bring it into being.

The paradox is that once brought into existence, organizations tend to lose this fire. We have myths about maturing businesses: They have to oust the entrepreneur and bring in professionals. They should institute controls and become more predictable. As a result, we take institutions that began as a freedom and turn them into fields of restraint, in the name of immortality and control in the form of scale.

In addition to the entrepreneurial instinct, another force works for freedom and exposes the arthritic quality of our institutions: the rapid changes in the economies of most Western countries. Large stable organizations are now at risk. Secure jobs are disappearing in most sectors. Free agency is replacing long-term employment. When large systems grow and shrink more quickly than ever, it reinforces the call to constantly recreate our lives and our institutions. The self-sovereignty movement is one, small version of the desire to find freedom and accountability in making a living and producing economic security. There are elements in this movement that contain the limitations of strong self-interest and the politics of anti-government. But this confusion between liberty and freedom is simply more evidence of our imperfect humanity. It gives an indication that there is energy among us to imagine that institutional forms and freedom are making eye contact.

Still, we need to acknowledge that our efforts to in fact create our future and live that out in our institutions runs counter to our wish for safety. The fad and follower instinct among organizations is stunning, even in a time of rapid change. You hear all the time that every organization wants to be a leader, but you see that they are only willing to try what has been proven elsewhere first.

"Whichever our resolve, whether to follow the Joneses or think for ourselves, it is, of course, not easy to make peace with the demands of our roles."

— *Peter Koestenbaum (1971)*

We participate in the search for evidence. A good thing as long as it does not overpromise. Evidence-based medicine and teaching should not be stamps of approval. Just helpful. And the shield of what the finance and legal departments say is also helpful but not a "truth." When we accept that we are constituting our world, we will be prepared to try things that are unproven. We will remember the existence of free will and will power. We might expect and demand that we, ourselves, provide the leadership that previously we sought in others. We will still experience anxiety and risk, but knowing they are inescapable makes them easier to endure. Add in that the conversations implied here end our isolation and helplessness. Eventually we will see anxiety and risk as the catalyst that brings us to life again and again. Granted, not a great value proposition.

If my freedom is a fact, and if I am accountable for what surrounds me, then what choice do I have but to move willingly into the fire of the marketplace? I find energy in creating organizations that are based on a philosophic, albeit somewhat tragic, sense of what it means to be a human being and a human system. And, with others in the same spot, we can create organizations that recognize and support our humanity rather than deny it.

Epilogue: Final Words from the Philosopher

An absolutely basic principle of our freedom is that all healing occurs in relationships. Although absolutes are always dangerous, it is safe to say that pure self-help is rare and what heals is the relationship between two or more persons. There are reasons for this. Authenticity often requires that we replace the suppressed premises by which we live. Transformation, in every case, puts aside our isolation. We need an encounter with other persons to affirm our humanity and sustain our intentions.

Central to these ideas is that words create a world. They are the action steps. Therefore, another essence of our freedom is our speech. We must use frequently and with full awareness of their meaning expressions such as "I choose . . . ." and "I am responsible for. . . ." in exchange for statements of what the world, or the culture, or that person has imposed on me. So that when we would otherwise be tempted to say, "They are depressing me," as if my depression is an effect of their actions, we must now say, "I am unable to cope with my experience of depression."

In using these expressions freely and repeatedly we are reminding ourselves of the intentional character of all experience. We thereby remain aware of the transcendental dimension of all experience. We recognize that every object—the feeling of depression in this case—is a form asking who is doing the speaking. When you say, "I am depressed" then you are a camera that shoots a wilted flower. But when you make your statement that way, you ignore the fact of the camera and all you recognize as real is the wilted flower. It is as if the subject and verb of the sentence did not exist—only the predicate. You are ignoring the "I am" of the sentence and seeing only the "depression" aspect.

The alternative is to take advantage of the world-constructing powers of our language. Our mode of speech must recognize that the depressed has an "I am" attached to it and that the wilted flower has a camera before it. This greater precision of language leads to a more accurate perception and conception of the world and will therefore be reflected as an improvement in our whole lifestyle. When we add to "I am" the idea that "I choose" and get "I am choosing to be depressed" (or better, "I am choosing not to deal with my depression") we clearly remind ourselves that being the subject and not the object is free. If we recognize that the camera is part of the wilted-flower complex, then we realize that it is the clicking of the shutter—which here symbolizes a free act—which produces the picture. In expanding our language in this way our mind increases in accuracy.

If it is true that language constructs experience, then we can expect that our life will develop a tendency to increasingly conform to the recognition of our freedom. Thus, by focusing also on the subjective dimension whenever we are in the presence of an emotional object, we maintain a clear awareness of our freedom. And that is precisely what we must do to cope with the anxiety of freedom.

The basic strategy of coping with the anxiety of freedom—that is, overcoming the paralysis brought about by the denial of freedom, by avoiding the confrontation with and integration of freedom—is taking the risk of action. We must learn to risk in small doses. By so doing we will gradually increase our toleration for the anxiety of freedom, and we will also be able to take advantage of the existence of freedom. Through risk we become aware that the anxiety of freedom can be tolerated, that freedom is our nature, and that it feels good to integrate the anxiety of freedom into our total personality. Risking effectively is an art that matures through experience.

Adapted from Peter Koestenbaum,
The New Image of the Person:
The Theory and Practice of Clinical Philosophy,
Westport, CT: Greenwood Publishing Co., 1978.

Finally, the concept of freedom is not a unitary idea but a blend—one which, to use Wittgenstein's famous example, consists of family resemblances. The concept of freedom is like a rope, held firmly together by many interweaving and overlapping strands without any single fiber running continuously throughout. These fibers are called "will," "consciousness," "ego," "self," "time," "spontaneity," "passivity," "autonomy," "self-determination," "action," "commitment," "engagement," "detachment," "distancing," and on and on.

Above all, in a philosophy of freedom there always exists the danger that the ideas of realistic limits and of instinctual behavior have not been adequately emphasized. Stress on free will can misguide one into thinking that this philosophy is relativistic, permissive, libertarian, and in general irresponsible, as well as super-rationalistic in the sense that our conscious and deliberate will controls all life. These misconceptions—especially the latter—must be rectified. . . .

In general, deep freedom does not mean omnipotence but rather withdrawal into the "nothingness" of consciousness—the "empty space" of awareness. In that nothingness the individual faces the infinite freedom to adopt definitions of self, organizations of experience such as a workplace, and attitudes toward social facts. While we are not free to change the objects of consciousness into something that they are not, we are free to use the laws of nature for control and technological rearrangement of objects.

In sum, understanding freedom means nothing without understanding responsibility and accountability. Responsibility means that every apparently minor choice is really a choice of grave and serious consequences, since each choice implies a complete definition of our nature and our world. Responsibility is the fact each of us is free, accountability is the individual act of accepting and choosing that fact. Furthermore, responsibility as an aspect of freedom is also the understanding that one of our earliest and most primitive choices is to recognize the real limits to our existence. If we choose our limits, then we connect with the world and are thereby healthy. If we deny them, then we sever ourselves from the world and are therefore sick. Even being free is itself a limit to human existence.

Adapted from Peter Koestenbaum,
*The Vitality of Death: Essays in Existential
Psychology and Philosophy,* Westport, CT:
Greenwood Publishing Co., 1971.

References and Background Reading

Berry, Wendell. *The Unsettling of America: Culture and Agriculture.* New York: Random House, 1982.

Berman, Marshall. *All That Is Solid Melts into Air: The Experience of Modernity*, 2nd ed. New York: Simon & Schuster, 1981. See also *Adventures in Modernism: Thinking with Marshall Berman*, edited by Jennifer Corby. New York: Terreform, 2016.

Block, Peter. *Community: The Structure of Belonging*, 2nd ed. Oakland, CA: Berrett-Koehler, 2018.

Esteva, Gustavo, Babones, Salvatore, Babcicky, Philipp. *The Future of Development: A Radical Manifesto*. Bristol, UK: Policy Press, 2013.

Edinger, Edward F. *Melville's Moby-Dick, An American Nekyia*, 2nd ed. Scarborough, ON: Inner City Books, 1995.

Frankl, Viktor. *Man's Search for Meaning: An Introduction to Logotherapy*. Translated by Ilse Lasch. Boston: Beacon Press, 2006, originally published 1946.

Hollis, James. *The Broken Mirror: Refracted Visions of Ourselves.* Asheville, NC: Chiron Publications, 2022.

Koestenbaum, Peter. *The New Image of the Person: Theory and Practice of Clinical Philosophy*. Westport, CT: Greenwood Press, 1978.

Koestenbaum, Peter. *The Vitality of Death: Essays in Existential Psychology and Philosophy*. Westport, CT: Greenwood Press, 1971.

Lupton, Robert D. *Toxic Charity: How Churches and Charities Hurt Those They Help, And How to Reverse It*. New York: HarperOne, 2011.

Sandel, Michael J. *The Tyranny of Merit: What's Become of the Common Good?* New York: Farrar, Straus and Giroux, 2020.

Villanueva, Edgar. *Decolonizing Wealth: Indigenous Wisdom to Heal Divides and Restore Balance,* 2nd ed. Oakland, CA: Berrett-Koehler, 2021.

Wood, Ellen Meiksins. *The Origin of Capitalism: A Longer View,* rev. ed. Brooklyn, NY: 2017.

Acknowledgments

It is very unusual for someone to study your earlier writings, consider them important, and then make the effort to bring them to a larger audience. That is what Peter Block has done here. He has selected the existential themes from my older books, culled from them what he deemed relevant, edited them for greater accessibility, and surrounded them with some very sensitive commentary.

It was important to him that he did it. It was even more important to me that he did it.

How can one properly acknowledge such an undertaking? It is a magical mixture of friendship, ethics, loyalty, responsibility, meaning, and service. It is a clarion call to my conscience, holding me accountable to be worthy for the remainder of my days of such faith in the viability of these ideas—which are our common human heritage. I have no choice but to accept the challenge and to honor it.

The hope is that here is a service. All of us are partners in life and whatever we can do to support one another will earn us our place under the sun. Plato taught us that all philosophic knowledge is recollection. Our joint reward

151

will be that you the reader will discover powers within you that will see you through some of the more difficult moments of life.

—Peter Koestenbaum

My fundamental acknowledgment is to Peter Koestenbaum. My life would have limped along even more than it has if not for an accidental encounter with him. More of this in the body of the book.

Also of essential importance is Leslie Stephen, who has made everything I write more readable and accessible. She instantly grasps what the book is about, is faithful to the author's voice, and cares deeply about the ideas. A rare combination. I keep writing because I know Leslie is present. I am grateful for the skill and insight Rebecca Taff brought to the research she did to get this book started. Also thanks to Maggie Rogers for making everything work with warmth and intelligence and skill.

My thanks also to Ken Murphy, who supported me and my work for years, and is now a friend bringing his gifts into the film and documentary world. Years ago Ken risked bringing the ideas of philosophy into a Humanities for Human Resources series at Philip Morris. We were nervous about this experiment, especially since we told participants that this was about ideas and we made no commitment that anything useful or actionable would be offered. Would anyone sign up? They did and thanked us for the experience. They said it was a welcome relief not to have to come up with a list of action step to make the trainers feel good. This was a moment in time where there was a place for reflection, depth, and thought in modern corporations.

I also want to thank Charles Holmes who has embraced innovative ideas for as long as I have known him. He is a master convener and created more than one occasion where Peter could bring his commitment and being into the world. Also Michael Murray who brought Peter and me to Dallas to spend two days exploring what philosophy has to offer executives and change agents in making the world more productive and habitable.

Thanks to Jim Block, my dear brother and amazing photographer. This is the second book cover of mine that he has brought to life with his work. He took about 40 images of water miraculously suspended in midair, which should be a book of its own.

The Wiley team has also been a delight to work with. Zach Schisgal, my editor, and Michelle Hacker, managing editor, have been supportive every step of the way. Editorial assistant Jozette Moses, including her team of designers, production editor Manikandan Kuppan, and copyeditor Sheryl Nelson make things happen, which is all that you want when you are eager to see a book to completion. Thank you all.

—*Peter Block*

About the Authors

Peter Block is an author, consultant, and citizen of Cincinnati, Ohio. His work is about chosen accountability and the reconciliation of community.

Peter is the author of several best-selling books. The most widely known are *Flawless Consulting: A Guide to Getting Your Expertise Used* (1st edition 1980, 4th edition 2023); *Stewardship: Choosing Service Over Self-Interest* (1993, 2nd edition 2013); and *The Empowered Manager: Positive Political Skills at Work* (1987, 2nd edition 2017).

Peter's newest book is co-authored with Walter Brueggemann and John McKnight, *An Other Kingdom: Departing the Consumer Culture,* published by Wiley in 2016. The books are about ways to create workplaces and communities that work for all. They offer an alternative to the patriarchal beliefs that dominate our culture. His work is to bring change into the world through consent and connectedness rather than through mandate and force.

Peter is founder of Designed Learning, a training company that offers workshops he designed to build the skills outlined in his books.

Peter served on the Board of Directors of LivePerson, a provider of online engagement solutions, and he has also served on Clifton Town Meeting, his local neighborhood council. He is director emeritus of Elementz, an urban arts center in Cincinnati. With other volunteers in Cincinnati, Peter began A Small Group, whose work is to create a new community narrative and to bring his work on civic engagement into being. Currently Peter is a part of Common Good Alliance, a Cincinnati effort to create everyday African American wealth by collectively owning and controlling land, housing, enterprise, and the arts in a local neighborhood.

Peter's office is in Mystic, Connecticut. You can visit his websites at peterblock.com and designedlearning.com. He welcomes being contacted at pbi@att.net.

Peter Koestenbaum has a consulting practice, going back twenty-five years, running seminars, giving lectures, and doing individual leadership coaching. He been close to business executives and their deepest concerns, sharing with them insights and feelings, new perspectives, and more serviceable adaptations.

His education was in physics, music, and above all philosophy, having earned degrees from Stanford (studying physics and philosophy), Harvard (studying philosophy), and Boston Universities (studying theology and philosophy)—(B.A., M.A., and Ph.D., respectively, all in philosophy), but also attending the University of California (Berkeley, in music and philosophy).

He taught for thirty-four years in the Philosophy Department of San Jose State University, in California, having received the Statewide Outstanding Professor Award.

While teaching, he spent twenty-five years working with psychologists and psychiatrists exploring the relationship between psychiatry and the healing potential of philosophy.

Peter decided to apply the insights he gained in philosophy and psychiatry to business: management, strategic thinking, marketing, but above all to leadership. His primary concern has been to develop philosophy-in-business as a bona fide profession, undergirding the use of the behavioral sciences in business—covering not only personal and cultural matters but also strategic and marketing topics.

This journey has taken him to more than forty countries in five continents. A sample of the companies with which he worked extensively includes Ford, IBM, Ciba-Geigy (now Novartis), Citibank, Volvo, Amoco, and Xerox. Peter was heavily involved with EDS—Electronic Data Systems—and with one of the large Korean *Chaebols*.

Peter can be reached through the Koestenbaum Institute, headquartered in Los Angeles and Stockholm, at rolf.falkenberg@telia.com, through the Philosophy-in-Business website: www.PiB.net (email: info@PiB.net), or through his email address at peter@koestenbaum.com.

"A Talk with the Remarkable Dr. Peter Koestenbaum" by Doug Kirkpatrick is comprehensive interview with Peter that can be accessed at https://medium.com/redshift-3/a-talk-with-the-remarkable-dr-peter-koestenbaum-f83f2b11 7433.

Index

159

𝕃 designedLearning®

Designed Learning, a Peter Block company, is committed to providing experiences to create workplaces and communities that work for the common good of all. At the center of the world of organizational change for more than thirty years, Designed Learning has trained over one million people in hundreds of countries worldwide based on Peter's best-selling books.

We invite you to explore the ideas in this book and Peter's work. We would love to connect with you. Designed Learning is a full-service training, consulting, and coaching company existing to help organizations and communities build a human culture of relatedness and connection through conversations to consult, convene, and empower all voices.

Visit our website at www.designedlearning.com or email us directly to explore the possibilities.

Website: www.designedlearning.com
Email: admin@designedlearning.com